ALL THREE PARTS
of the *GLASS HALF-FULL ADOPTION MEMOIRS series*

OpenAdoption OpenHeart Arms & Mind

an adoptive father's
inspiring true story

RUSSELL ELKINS

Open Adoption, Open Heart, Arms and Mind:
An Adoptive Father's Inspiring True Story
all three books in the Glass Half-Full Adoption Memoirs series
By Russell Elkins
©2019 Russell Elkins

Some of the names in this book have been changed to protect the privacy of the individuals involved.

Chief line editor books 1 & 2: Kim Foster
Chief line editor book 3: Jenna Lovell
Content editors: Martin Casey, Cathy Watson Childs, Kim Foster, Jenna Lovell

Cover photos and author photo by Jammie Elkins Photography
Cover design by Inky's Nest Design
Interior book layout by Inky's Nest Design

ISBN: 978-1-950741-03-8

Inky's Nest Publishing

RussellElkins.com
1st edition
First edition printed in 2019 in the United States of America

BOOK ONE of the *GLASS HALF-FULL ADOPTION MEMOIRS series*

To my beautiful wife, Jammie.
The best mother and partner I could have possibly hoped for.

CONTENTS

Open Adoption
Open Heart

CONTENTS

Open Adoption
OpenArms

CONTENTS

INTRODUCTION 1

ADOPTION, A MODERN PERSPECTIVE

When I was a young child in the 1980s and my family lived in South Carolina, our next-door neighbors adopted a baby boy. It was not too long afterward that the Navy transferred our family to California and we quickly lost contact with all of our South Carolina friends. Twenty-five years later, when my brother, Clark, found himself visiting South Carolina again, he went to our old neighborhood to take pictures of things he remembered from his childhood. While he was standing in the street in front of our old house, a young man from next door came out to see what he was up to. Clark realized immediately who this young man was and started to talk about the exciting day when his parents first brought him home.

"It was a lot of fun. The whole block was invited to the party," Clark said.

The young man shook his head, "I think you have me confused with someone else. I wasn't adopted."

"Oh," Clark said. "I just assumed since you look like you're in your twenties that the math lined up. It must have been a family that lived there before."

"No. My parents have owned this house for over thirty years. They have been the only ones to live here for that long."

"Well, then you have to be the guy."

"No. That's not me. I'm not adopted."

"Yeah, but..." Clark cut off his words when he noticed his wife squeezing his hand much tighter than usual and glanced over to see the look she was giving him. "Oh. Right. I must be thinking of someone else," and he quickly changed the subject.

Clark had only been six years old when we lived in South Carolina, so he had to wonder if his memory was incorrect. He called our parents when he got home that evening and, sure enough, he just had to be that adopted baby boy.

Clark felt terrible.

People did not typically speak as openly about adoption in the 1980s as they do now.

My wife and I knew very little about adoption when we first began to entertain the idea. We had wrongfully assumed that it was pretty much the same as when we were kids—when it was common to refrain from talking about it. It was not until we attended our first adoption orientation that we were introduced to the concept of "open adoption."

The terms "open" and "closed" adoption can have different meanings for different people. Typically, a closed adoption means the adoption agency (or someone else) decides on which home the child is to be placed. The biological parents and the adoptive family have no contact with each other.

Open adoption is a broad term that means there has been some level of contact between the biological parents and the adoptive family. In some cases, open adoption means the biological parents choose the couple without ever personally meeting them. In others, it can mean there is regular contact, such as exchanging photographs or visiting face-to-face.

Open adoption emerged in the late 1970s and early 1980s, but the idea was still considered radical. Few adoption agencies offered this option because many people still viewed the practice as an ongoing experiment. They did not know how this practice would affect the biological parents, adoptive parents, adopted children, or the adoption agency itself.

In many cases, the new concept of open adoption proved to be beneficial for all people involved. In studies done in the late 1980s and early 1990s, teenagers from open adoptions reported that they enjoyed having a larger support group (both adoptive family and biological family), felt they were more comfortable with their personal identity, and had a greater desire to know more about their biological family than did those who were adopted through closed adoption.

Caseworkers began to see the benefits of open adoption, but influence from biological parents was the biggest factor in agencies making open adoptions popular. Biological parents enjoyed the ability to help choose the home in which their child would be placed. They also enjoyed having a say in what type of contact they could have with the adoptive family after placement. And by the time the mid-1990s came around, it was more common for biological parents to choose to place their children with agencies that offered open adoptions rather than with those that did not.

Agencies that did not make the change struggled to stay afloat. With less biological parents choosing those agencies, the number of children placed through those agencies dropped. Also, upon seeing that birthparents preferred open adoption, adoptive couples became open to the new idea. The change was quick, and by the turn of the twenty-first century, open adoption had become the norm rather than the exception.

The concept of having contact with the biological parents was foreign to my wife and me as we began considering adoption, but as we discussed the pros and cons with our caseworker, we rather easily made the decision to choose open rather than closed adoption. We had decided long before we even first stepped into the agency office that we wanted to raise our child to embrace his or her roots rather than keep them secret (as was the case with that young man in South Carolina). We wanted our children to grow up proud of where they came from, and the concept of open adoption fit perfectly into that plan. We have never regretted our decision.

It was not quite as simple and easy as we thought it would be, though. Before a child is born, the biological parents have the only say in what happens with that child. That means that a couple hoping to adopt has the right to do little more than that: hope. Even if the hopeful adoptive couple is contacted early in the pregnancy, the biological parents have every right to change their mind about placing their child until formalities are finalized through the court system. That can be quite the stressful ride for an adoptive couple since almost all people who consider placing a child for adoption will second-guess their decision throughout the entire process.

Once an adoption is finalized, however, those tables turn.

After the biological parents dissolved their parental rights, the adoptive couple now holds all the power in the relationship. Most adoption agencies urge adoptive couples and biological parents to come to an agreement before the adoption takes place about the type of contact that will exist after placement. Some states even require that agreement in writing before the adoption can be finalized. But even if that agreement is reached, there are no legal ramifications if the adoptive parents go back on their part of the deal.

The difficulty lies in the fact that neither party really knows what they are getting into when they discuss the details of their agreement. Most of the time neither side had ever been in this position before. Even if they had, every adoption relationship is unique. These people typically know very little about one another when the adoption takes place and have had very little time to form what will end up being a very intense relationship.

Because of these factors along with many more, biological and adoptive parents often feel insecure until they figure out the new relationship. And even when they do a good job figuring out their relationship, aspects of that relationship often change quickly in an open adoption.

My wife and I would find ourselves facing internal battles we had not anticipated. It is not human nature to want to share the idea of parenthood with someone else. But we were determined to make our relationships work. We were determined not to be one of those couples who cut ties with our child's biological family just because things got tough.

Our road proved to be very bumpy and difficult, but it was also very much worth the ride. We would not change a thing if we could. It is the best thing that has ever happened to us. My wife and I are even closer now than we were before because we have learned new levels of love—both toward our child and toward our child's birth family. We embrace our roles as adoptive parents, and do not wish we had it any different. We love our unique family tree. We are proud of our family and hope to instill that same pride in our child. What a wonderful world we have discovered with open adoption!

1-1

FRUSTRATIONS WITH INFERTILITY

When my wife, Jammie, and I were first married, we used birth control. We were not waiting for anything specific before starting our family, but we did not want to start right away. As is the case with many newlywed couples, many people thought it was their place to give us unsolicited advice about when we should start having children. Some thought we should start immediately, and others told us we were crazy if we did not wait at least a few years.

About six months after we were married, while I was still in college, we decided to stop using contraceptives. We were not necessarily "trying" to start our family at that time, but we were happy to become parents if God sent a child to us. As the months went by, we gradually went from wondering if it would happen to hoping it would. It didn't happen.

After being married for about a year-and-a-half, I graduated from college and we moved to Boise, Idaho. We bought a house. We both started new jobs and began making friends. We were starting a new chapter in our life, and we began to really yearn to become parents. We started to try out some of the advice others had given us—even some things that were probably more superstitions and old wives tales than anything else. It didn't work.

Jammie started to keep a log of everything her body did. She kept a thermometer handy to take her temperature. She paid close attention to when her body felt unusual. She monitored everything she was expecting to happen. She took her blood pressure throughout each month. She wrote all of her observations in a small notebook she kept with her at all times. None of this seemed to help.

We started to play mind games with ourselves. We interpreted things the way we wanted them to be, thinking that any change in Jammie's body temperature or sickness in the morning might mean we were finally pregnant. Still, whether her period started early, on time, or late, the bad news always came.

Unpleasant feelings that accompany difficult situations usually soften with time, but that did not happen for us with infertility. With each month of disappointment, we did not become more accustomed to it. Quite the contrary, actually. Every month intensified our disappointment. We played more mind games with ourselves, trying to understand what we were doing so wrong to make God unwilling to send us a child.

It was not a secret around our social circles that we were struggling with this. Most people at work and those living on our street knew. Everybody at church knew our situation.

The problem was not that everybody knew, nor was it that so many people wanted to be sympathetic and help. The problem was that few people knew how to make us feel more comfortable in our situation. Some people avoided the topic all together, but many tried too hard to empathize.

Every year a handful of men at church would pressure me, trying to get me to go to a father-and-son campout. I did not want to go because I would either feel like I was camping alone or intruding on someone else's father-and-son time.

Each year on Mother's Day, Jammie would try to slip out of church quickly before someone could corner her, but every year people would track her down, thinking they were helping her feel better by pressuring her into receiving a flower.

Naturally, some people struggling with infertility would be hurt if they were not given a flower on Mother's Day or invited to a campout. Every couple reacts differently to the situation, and it is almost impossible for others to know how to act. What works for one couple may not be a good idea with another. There is no easy solution.

We did have a small group of people whom we allowed to be our true sympathizers. It was nice to have them along for the ride, even if they had never been in our shoes. They prayed with us. They hoped with us. They hurt with us. All were really close friends or relatives, but few of whom had actually struggled with infertility.

One of Jammie's friends who did relate was Natalie. Not only had she been told she would never be able to have children, but she was also a nurse at a fertility clinic. She spent her day at work helping people just like us. Jammie and Natalie were able to confide in one another. The biggest blessing of all, though, was that she shared her expertise. It was nice to receive advice from someone who knew the science of infertility, and had valuable experience instead of the well-intentioned, yet unsolicited, advice from people who thought the only reason for our infertility was because we ate the wrong foods.

We resisted visiting Natalie's office for a long time. Each month we ached and suffered from another month of infertility, but we still were hesitant. Finally, while out on one of our many walks, Jammie and I talked about how big of a blessing it was to have Natalie in our life, and we wondered why we were not taking advantage of the situation. I was reminded of the popular allegory where floods came and a man on his roof prayed for God to save him. Along came a boat, which he turned away, saying God was going to come save him. Then the same thing happened with a helicopter. After he drowned, he asked God in heaven why He did not come to save him, and God corrected him, saying that He sent the boat and helicopter. Jammie and I were sitting there, waiting for God to send us a baby the same way children come to most everyone else, but He was sending us a different lifeline. We were being stubborn, waiting for things to be done our own way, and on our own timetable. That is not how God works.

I got myself checked out first because we had been told it is a good idea to get the male's sperm tested early because it is an easy problem to diagnose.

I was pretty nervous about the visit because I thought that I was going to have to give a sperm sample in a public building. I pictured myself stuck at the doctor's office for hours while people knocked on the door asking if I was all right. I was relieved when they gave me the option of taking the test at home.

The test came out clean and healthy. But, was that good news or bad news? I suppose it was nice to know nothing was wrong with my body, but at the same time, it did not make us feel like we were any closer to solving our problem.

One positive thing that came out of it all was that I was able to give serious thought to how I would feel if I were to find out my body was the problem. I always told Jammie I would not look at her differently if we discovered that her body was preventing pregnancy, and I have never wavered from that. Waiting for my test results to come back solidified that way of thinking for me.

Jammie began her visits with Natalie by getting an ultrasound. Just like with my sperm test, her ultrasound showed that everything seemed healthy. Again, was that supposed to be good news? We were hoping to find some answers so we could either take a pill or inject some medicine, and the problem would be solved. Telling us that we were healthy just made us feel stuck in our progression.

Natalie got Jammie started on a series of shots to help boost the chances of getting pregnant. These shots also increased the likelihood that we could end up with twins or triplets. By that point, we were not too worried about the number, as long as we could have children. At that time, we had no real concept of how much work it would have been to have more than one baby. Yes, we were pretty naïve.

When the end of that first month came, we were on pins and needles. We knew which day Jammie was supposed to start her period, and we hoped it would not happen. It did. Still, just like had done before we started the specialized treatments, we tortured ourselves by wasting a few home pregnancy tests just to make sure.

During the second month—and I was not entirely sure why—I found myself having "that feeling." I felt convinced *this month is the month!* Natalie's magical shots were going to work. I was sure of it. I was convinced that Jammie was going to be carrying a little person inside of her after that month. I felt confident about it all month...up until her next period proved me wrong. As it turned out, my feelings were more desperation than inspiration.

The second month of treatments should have been easier on us emotionally since we had already been through the heartache once. It should have been, but it was not. It seemed reasonable to assume we would succeed during that second month since it was supposed to work that first month. Our emotional crash at the end of the second month was worse than that of the first.

We began the third month of shots. This time Jammie was much more optimistic than I was, though I did my best to keep that pessimism to myself. When her period came at the end of the month, even though I still hoped more than anything that I was wrong, I did not expect her to be pregnant this time. Again, the treatments did not work.

It was hard for me to swallow. There we were, sitting on the roof in the heavy rain. A boat came to save us from drowning. God had clearly sent us a lifeline, but I guess it was leaking or broken because it did not work. That did not make any sense. The ultrasounds and tests always told us everything was ideal for the treatments to work. I had felt so confident when we started the process that I was already making parental plans in my head. After all, we were not hoping for something unusual. We just wanted to do what many couples accomplish by accident. Still, after a few months of trying harder than ever before, and thus building up our hopes more than ever before, we were still stuck in the same place we had always been—just the two of us with only our two dogs to keep us company.

We had some decisions to make. Many people repeat the same process over and over and sometimes have results farther down the road, but we opted out. Three months of receiving the shots might not sound like a very long time, but when we were going through it, it felt like a decade. I admit our decision had a little to do with being somewhat strapped for cash, but if we had felt like it was the right road for us, we would have found a way. We definitely would have found a way.

We spent a lot of time on our knees in prayer, and we took a lot of walks together to talk things over. We felt it was time to jump ship and move on to something else. Years of infertility, topped off with some unsuccessful treatments, left us hungry for something different. There were plenty of other infertility treatments we could have tried, but we were finished. We were worn out. Each month made it harder and harder, and we felt like the road we were on was not leading us anywhere.

All of our friends had been excited when we started visiting Natalie's clinic. When we decided not to continue our treatments, however, some of those same friends were not too happy with us. Some people radiated their disapproval. They talked to us differently after that point, like we were foolish for quitting so quickly. One thing about personal revelation, though, is that it is personal. Jammie and I were in charge of our own situation, and we knew we were making the right decision for us.

Trials in life can sometimes be difficult to understand while we are right in the thick of things. In retrospect, I can now see how those trying times helped make us stronger. And even more important than that, looking back I can see how important those months were in helping us prepare for one of our true callings in life—being adoptive parents. Those hard times helped us to not only become ready to adopt, but to become *excited* to adopt.

1-2

THE QUEST FOR ADOPTION

I imagine that the decision to shift focus from infertility treatments to adoption would be a tough one for many couples, but it was not for us. When we talked about more infertility treatments, we felt exhausted and pessimistic. When we thought about adoption, those feelings changed to excitement and optimism. There was no glorious "aha" moment for us. It just felt natural to go with the option that brought us comfort and hope. And if the truth be told, I think part of the reason the prospect felt so much more comforting was because we thought it was going to be more predictable and promising. We soon found out that adoption is anything but predictable.

We began telling our friends about our change of plans, and about our newfound excitement for adoption. Many of those friends shared our enthusiasm, but there were others who thought we were "giving up" on having natural-born children.

They looked at our decision like we were settling for the next best thing, while we saw it as equally wonderful.

Some friends gave us suggestions of new things to try, making us feel as though they were hoping to save us from having to resort to adoption. They had a hard time understanding that we did not want to continue with any more miraculous medical procedures. We did not want try a new special diet that was sure to cure our infertility. We were not interested in using a surrogate mother. Our focus was now on one thing—adoption.

Most of our close friends paralleled our excitement, but not all. These friends viewed our glass as half empty rather than half full, while we chose to see our glass as filled to the brim. Once we decided that adoption right for us, we became excited almost overnight.

We chose an adoption agency, and attended a small orientation class. That was where we learned about open adoption for the first time. Even though we were not familiar with the term "open adoption," the concept made sense to us. We decided from the very beginning that an open adoption would be right for us.

In our orientation meeting, we learned about the requirements for adoptive couples, both with the agency as well as with the state. When we asked how long the process usually took, we were told that it depended upon how long it would take for expecting parents to choose us. Some couples get chosen within weeks while others wait five years or more.

The mountains of paperwork were tedious, but we worked hard on them and hammered it all out in about a month. It could have easily taken us much longer if we were not as motivated as we were. A caseworker came to our home to do our "homestudy," to make sure our house was safe and ideal for a child. We had our fingerprints and backgrounds checked. Jammie and I both got physicals from our local doctor. We shared our financial records with the agency. All of these things were done to show we were capable, ready, and trustworthy enough to take on a child.

Different states and adoption agencies have different requirements. With our situation, along with our paperwork and home inspection, we had to complete ten education hours. We attended local classes. We watched videos and read articles about the topics that most interested us. We traveled to an adoption convention in a different state where we completed more hours than we were required. We were so excited about adoption that we soaked in as much information as we could.

My greatest fear with the adoption process was the thought of coping with a failed placement. It pained me to think of becoming emotionally attached to a child, or getting my hopes up high, and then having something fall through. We attended a class that dealt with that very subject. I hoped the class would somehow reassure me and calm that fear, but I actually left it feeling worse than I did beforehand. I became more aware how common it is for adoptions to fall through. Our instructor had been through three such incidents, and she said that the feelings were very much the same as the times she had miscarriages with her natural pregnancies.

With all of our education hours completed, and after receiving approval from the agency and caseworker, our last step was to get our profile posted on the adoption agency's website. We spent a lot of time trying to get it just right. (I have included that letter at the end of this book for those interested in reading it)

We noticed that almost all of the couples' profile pictures were headshots. We did not want to look like just another couple. We wanted to stand out. Instead of a headshot, we wanted a picture that showed a little of our personalities. We chose to use a picture that showed us with our favorite hobbies—Jammie with her camera, and me with my acoustic guitar. We put a silly polka dot border around the picture to draw attention to it as well. Whether someone thought the polka dots were cheesy or not, we didn't care. Our goal was to catch someone's eye, and if that meant we needed to be cheesy then we were okay with that.

With our profile now online, all we could do now was to wait and hope. Having just finished so many hours of classes and mounds of paperwork, it was strange not to have anything to do. We used social media and other forms of communication to spread the word that we were adopting. We did have some thoughtful friends tell us they recommended us to someone considering adoption, but none of those referrals turned into anything. All we could do was wait.

Jammie and I believe very strongly in the power of prayer. At that time, my responsibilities at church were with the teenage boys, and Jammie worked with the teenage girls. We both spent a lot of time teaching and doing activities with the youth, so one Sunday we asked them if they wanted to help take part in a special day of prayer and fasting with us, specifically to help us with the blessing of being able to start our family. These young boys and girls were all very enthusiastic about being part of it, which made us feel very loved. When others also heard about our plan, they joined in as well.

My brother, Clark, and his family were the people closest to the whole situation. Clark is just eighteen months older than I am, and we grew up doing everything together. He moved here to Idaho and now lives just a few blocks away. He and his wife, Beth, had ached with us through our infertility, and they longed for the day when we could become parents almost as much as we did.

One day, about the time we finished our paperwork, they asked us to follow them into a separate room so we could talk in private. Jammie and I immediately suspected they were pregnant, and we were right. As was the case with most all of our friends, they were nervous to tell us, especially since, while it was a happy surprise for them, they were not trying for a fifth child when it happened.

I doubt they were worried we might be angry or resent them. However, they were justified in thinking we might be jealous or sad about someone else becoming pregnant. If this news had come to us a few months earlier, that may have been the case—although we would have still been excited for them.

Since we felt confident that were already on our own path to becoming parents, my brain quickly calculated the math. We were not only okay with the thought of someone else getting what we wanted, but we were also really excited about the idea that there was a chance we could have a child close in age to theirs. We smiled when we thought about these two kids possibly growing up together, stealing each other's toys, and knocking each other down. What could possibly be better than that?

1-3

THE LONG-AWAITED LETTER

Waiting was so very hard. The subject of adoption was never more than a millimeter from our minds. Every time we took one of our many walks, or while we ate dinner together, we could not seem to talk about anything else. It completely consumed us, similar to when we were trying the infertility treatments.

It was not happening as quickly as we wanted. Of course, our hopes of a quick process were not very reasonable. The average wait with our agency was about two years, and we had only been waiting a few months.

As if our need to wait was not painful enough, Jammie one day decided to hop onto the adoption agency's website to see how long it would take for our profile to show up. The agency we were using was a large one with hopeful adoptive couples all over the nation. We were heartbroken when our profile came up as number 851 out of 921 couple profiles. All of a sudden, we felt like small fish in a very big ocean. How could someone possibly choose us? How would they ever find us? Our hope of having a child close in age to my brother's baby suddenly felt impossible. We felt completely helpless again, just like when infertility treatments let us down.

Less than a week after Jammie had done that search something happened that changed everything. We suddenly didn't feel so hopeless anymore. We were no longer such small fish.

We got contacted by an expecting mother!

We were thrilled.

The e-mail she sent was short and simple, and it read like this:

Hi, My name is Brianna. I am 15 years old. I live in Mississippi and I am almost five months pregnant. I was looking at profiles and yours kind of jumped out at me. I have always wanted a baby and it hurts to have to give that up, even if it is my own decision. I know I can't give it what it needs when it comes to having both parents, and I have to do what is best for my baby. Anyway, I would love to talk to y'all about maybe adopting. Please e-mail me back.

Thank you, Brianna

Words cannot describe our feelings. Jammie was beside herself with excitement, but I was hesitant. I guess I tend to be the kind of guy who thinks that if it sounds too good to be true, it probably is. I do not like getting my hopes up just to be shut down, so my brain went quickly to pessimist mode.

I wondered if we were the only couple she had contacted. I knew that if I were in her position, I might contact a few different couples, and then choose between them.

I also wondered if there was a scammer on the other end of this e-mail just claiming to be a fifteen-year-old girl. Most adoptions take place within the biological parents' home state, so being contacted by someone outside of Idaho caused me to feel suspicious. Plus, we had heard a few horrible stories about how adoptive parents are purposefully led along, giving gifts and money, only for the potential birthparents to have a change of heart after a lot of hospital bills and expenses were paid for. Fortunately, there are laws in place to protect hopeful adoptive couples from that type of thing, but it still happens.

We wanted to write Brianna back immediately, but we were nervous that we would say the wrong thing. We decided to ask our caseworker, Jon, for advice. His initial thoughts were similar to mine. Even without telling him about my concerns, he wondered if it was a scam. He told us to go ahead and reply to her e-mail, and he would investigate into the background of the situation.

Jammie and I both wrote separate e-mails, and sent them together. We wanted her to see our individual personalities as well as show her that we were both interested and invested in this adoption.

Not long after sending her the e-mails, Jon called us back. He had talked to some caseworkers in charge of the agency in Mississippi, and there was not anybody named Brianna on their list of expecting mothers. We felt let down, but Jon counseled us not to worry because it was common for an expecting mother to contact a hopeful adoptive couple from their website before contacting the agency.

Brianna replied to us within a few hours, and we exchanged a few more e-mails the same day. We had been advised by people to keep our last names a secret—at least for a little while—but that secret was blown after just a few e-mails when we accidentally left our last name and contact information at the bottom of a letter. Oops. The next thing we knew, Brianna found us on Facebook and requested a link to our personal pages. We were excited and nervous all at the same time.

A lot of people also advised us to keep some emotional distance between us and the expecting parents, but even though it had only been a few hours since she first contacted us, we found ourselves excited to connect with her through Facebook anyway. We did, and that was where we got to see a picture of her for the first time. I was surprised when I saw her photo. For some reason, and I do not know why, I was expecting her to be African-American. For months I had been having a recurring dream in which we would adopt an African-American boy. The dreams felt so real that I guess I came to expect it to become true, and I was surprised when she turned out to be Caucasian. I was not glad or disappointed in the change—it was just different.

34

Not only were we able to look through her Facebook profile, but we also spent a few hours chatting on Facebook's instant messenger.

We discussed some things she needed to do in order to get in contact with the adoption agency. She soon did, and a Mississippi caseworker contacted Jon shortly afterward.

The situation was real. It was exciting. Both Jammie and I hardly slept that night. We rolled and tossed and turned. I am usually a really good sleeper, but I actually slept better the night before Jammie and I got married than I did that night.

We were too excited to keep this news a secret. We immediately started telling our friends, and the news spread like wildfire among everybody we knew. In no time at all, everyone around us buzzed with excitement.

The spark from Brianna's first letter ignited us in every way. Over the next few weeks her letters and words continued to feed the fire, but as time went on, we could see those flames slowly burning out. After only a month had gone by, we were left with just embers. Everything on her end was becoming increasingly more complicated, and it did not look like the adoption would happen. We eventually lost hope.

Even though we had our hopes up so high, the loss came so gradually that the pain was not nearly as severe as stories we had heard, nor could we say it compared to a natural birth miscarriage like others talked about. Still, we were sad. We were back to square one with just our two dogs to keep us company.

Brianna had tried to discuss adoption with the biological father, Daren, but he did not want to hear it. He was more interested in discussing marriage and raising the child together, but at age fifteen Brianna did not feel ready to be a wife and a mother. Neither of them wanted to budge from their position, and they found themselves at an impasse.

Brianna soon broke up with him, but Daren was not yet ready to let their relationship go. The only time he was willing to talk about the baby was when he was trying to use it as leverage to convince her to come back to him. When she refused to rekindle the relationship, he turned on her, spread rumors about her and sent her nasty e-mails.

Even when he seemed to have given up on rekindling his relationship with Brianna, he still refused to consider adoption. He made no attempt to help her with the pregnancy, whether emotionally or financially. He showed no interest in the child. In essence, he was telling her that he had no interest in caring of the child himself, but he wanted to be able to observe from a distance.

Without both signatures, the state of Mississippi would not allow Brianna to choose adoption. Brianna was the youngest of her siblings, and the last one still living at home. Her father lived on the other side of town, and her mother's job kept her out of the home most of the time, usually working through the night. Since she was not willing to marry Daren, it looked like the only choice for Brianna was to drop out of high school to raise this child on her own.

What a situation to be in! As sad and disappointed as Jammie and I were, Brianna was even more heartbroken. She was a straight-A student with plans of college and aspirations of someday becoming a nurse, but she found herself painted into a corner. She refused to even consider an abortion, so she had no other choice but to put those dreams on hold.

When we were first contacted by Brianna, our friends were so excited for us that the news had spread like wildfire. Once things fizzled out, we found that our friends were not so quick to spread the word. It seemed like every person in our social circle wanted an update, and we had to retell our bad news everywhere we went.

We were back to the drawing board—back to where we found ourselves as couple 851 out of 921 amazing profiles.

How frustrating.

1-4

BACK TO THE DRAWING BOARD

Very soon after we lost hope in our situation with Brianna, my cousin, Radene, called me. She was living in Pittsburgh, and she told me about a conversation her husband just had with their friend, Melissa. Melissa was a single mother in her 30s who just found out she was pregnant for a second time, and she was considering adoption for this child. Radene directed her to our personal blog, and gave her our email address.

Melissa soon reached out to us, and here is part of the e-mail she sent us:

> *I have known for a long time that this was not my baby to keep. I mean, I kept my daughter when she was born, even though I knew she wouldn't have a father in her life. I'm glad I made that decision and I stand by it, but still, this time it's different. I've pretty much known all along*

that this baby was meant for someone else. I know that— and not just because I have always felt a little guilty that my daughter doesn't have a father to help raise her.

Still, even though I knew this baby wasn't going to be ours to keep, I've been hesitant about something. I chose a couple in Kentucky that I liked, but I haven't been able to commit to them and now I think I know why. After talking to Justin and reading your profile online, I now feel that you are supposed to be my child's parents. I wondered for so long why I couldn't feel right about making the decision, and now I know. I'm so glad Justin introduced me to you guys.

It's hard to really get to know a couple by reading their profile. I mean, how can I really know if people are being honest just by reading something they wrote? Every couple's profile makes them look so wonderful. So with you guys, it's nice to know that Justin and Radene have known you for so long, and I trust what they say.

I have some questions for you about how open you want the adoption to be. Is it okay if we have some contact? We won't be intrusive—just some pictures would be nice— and let us write a letter to the child once in a while, too. And Jammie, I was wondering if you would like to be in the delivery room when the child is born. Also, would you like to know the sex of the child once I find out?

I look forward to hearing from you soon. You are an answer to my prayers. Melissa

We wrote back with a few questions, and waited for her response. It had been a little more than a month since Brianna first contacted us. Even though Melissa's letter seemed more definite and promising, Jammie and I did not feel quite the same level of excitement we had with Brianna's email. Was it because this was not our first time receiving contact? Or was it because we were protecting our emotions from more disappointment? Perhaps it was from another reason altogether.

Everything with Melissa made more sense when looking at it from a distance. Her letter showed us how firm she was in her conviction. It felt good to have something that appeared so solid. Still, for some reason, Jammie and I felt drawn to Brianna. I felt bad about having those thoughts. There we were, likely to become parents because of Melissa's selflessness, but for some reason we still found ourselves thinking about Brianna more than Melissa.

Brianna contacted us again. We had never stopped interacting with each other, but since the situation seemed hopeless and our options limited, we mentally resigned ourselves to the thought that she would raise the child. When she wrote us this time, she told us she was soon to get an ultrasound, and would then find out the baby's sex. Most interestingly, she still talked like she was hoping to find a way to make this adoption happen. She would not give up, so we continued to hold on to a small piece of hope, even though we could not see how she could convince Daren to sign the papers.

On the other hand, Melissa was planning to place a child with us as well. We did not know what to do, so we just waited.

There was not much else we could do. We did not want to rush into any major decisions. What would happen if we told both expecting mothers that we wanted both babies? We could possibly end up with two babies, just weeks apart, which would be almost like having twins. Or we could possibly scare both expecting mothers away.

It felt like a long time before we made any kind of decision, but it was only a few days. Brianna wrote us again and told us about her ultrasound. She bought us a nice card, which she sent to us through the postal service along with the ultrasound picture. The results were not completely clear, but they believed this child was going to be a boy.

Brianna's due date was moved up a whole month after the ultrasound. Not only was the baby arriving much earlier than previously expected, but the new due date was the exact same day that Clark and Beth were expecting their baby to be born. Melissa's baby was due about a month later than that.

Our emotions were all over the place, so we set up another meeting with Jon, our caseworker. He was well experienced in dealing with a lot of crazy situations, but ours was new to him. Normally, after an adoptive couple is contacted and chosen by an expecting mother, their adoption profile is removed from the agency's web page so they are not chosen again. Our situation with Brianna had never been solid enough to have our profile taken down, and our second contact was from an inside contact, so we were in a unique position. Jon discussed it with some influential people within the agency, and they ultimately decided we could adopt both babies as long as both expecting mothers were both okay with the idea.

We were not sure how we wanted to go about asking Brianna and Melissa. In fact, we were not really sure we could even handle two babies. We did feel, however, that the problem would probably iron itself out. Brianna's situation seemed hopeless with Daren's refusal to sign, and there was nothing anybody was going to be able to do about it. Plus, we still felt confident that Melissa was going to place her baby with us. That would be that. Everything would work itself out, right?

It was not that easy.

We decided to first ask Brianna what she thought about us adopting both babies. We wanted to ask her first because if we were going to scare someone off, we figured it might as well be the expecting mother with the impossible legal issues. If it scared her away, then it was never meant to be, and we would not even have to bother Melissa about it.

Our question did not scare Brianna away, though. Actually, she was really excited about the possibility. She loved to think her baby would have a sibling so close in age.

We then wrote Melissa an e-mail and waited. We could not do much more than wait since everything hung on what she would want to do.

She did not write us back.

We wrote a few other letters in hopes of getting something in return, but Melissa never did write us back. We called my cousin, Radene, to see if she knew what was going on, but she never had any new information. Even though Melissa was so convinced in her first e-mail that we were the right couple for her child, she changed her mind. We were not sure if it was our question that scared her off, but she chose to place her child with a different couple. She never did write us back.

Since our situation seemed to be drastically different every week, our friends were always ready for an update. Our life was not usually so dramatic. One minute Brianna wanted us to parent her child, and then she did not have a choice. Next, Melissa wanted us to raise her child—then they both wanted us—then just Brianna. If I had not already gone bald, I am sure my hair would have fallen out.

Even though Jammie and I doubted the adoption would take place, Brianna still held onto her hopes. She still hoped to figure something out.

Then someone suggested she look into the adoption laws for Idaho where Jammie and I live. Laws vary from state-to-state, and Idaho has different regulations than Mississippi. In Idaho, the biological father cannot stop an adoption by simply refusing to sign the papers. In Idaho, if he is not interested in parenting the child himself, he could not stop her from choosing adoption. Most importantly, if the baby was born in Idaho, then the situation would be subject to the laws of Idaho, not of Mississippi.

Brianna discussed the possibilities with her mother and caseworker, and the next news we received blew us away.

Brianna was coming to Idaho. And since her doctor did not want her traveling during the last two months of her pregnancy, she would be arriving in less than a week!

1-5

SOLVING A BIG PROBLEM

Brianna was coming to our home state of Idaho to have her baby. She was only fifteen-years-old, and had never traveled very far away from home—especially not without the accompaniment of an adult. Since her mother's job would not allow her to come until shortly before the baby was due, Brianna would be traveling alone.

Brianna had never flown in a plane. Through the generosity of a friend who worked for an airline, Jammie and I had access to some standby tickets. We did have to still pay for the tickets, but they were at a significantly reduced price, which was a wonderful blessing. But standby tickets posed some new challenges that made us nervous. Our local Boise airport is somewhat small, and there were no direct flights all the way here. We did not want her to have to worry about connecting flights or other complications for an inexperienced flyer (especially since it was close to Christmas), so we booked a one-way flight to the nearest big city, Salt Lake City, Utah, which was a five hour drive away, and we went to pick her up there.

Brianna had a cell phone, but at the time her plane was supposed to land, our attempts to call went straight to voicemail. Naturally, our minds started to rummage through all the possibilities of what could have gone wrong. Did her standby tickets get her bumped to a different flight than we first expected? Was she still up in the air somewhere and that was why her phone was off? If so, how would we know when she was going to land? How would we ever find her? We had seen a few photos of her, but we were not positive we would recognize her when we saw her in person.

Since Brianna was a minor, Jammie received permission from the airline to meet her at the arrival gate. She set off to search for her while I waited near the baggage claim area. We figured she would stand out, so Jammie wandered the terminals until she found someone who resembled Brianna's photo—a young pregnant teenager standing alone. When she asked her name, she was not Brianna. What were the odds of that happening?

Jammie abandoned her search and joined me near the baggage claim area. From our vantage point we could not see the top of the escalator, so each passenger appeared gradually as they descended. As the congestion of travelers began to thin out, we saw a lone female passenger begin to descend wearing a pair of warm winter boots. Her pregnant belly then appeared.

Finally, the face we clearly recognized from her photographs came into view. This time we did not have to ask her name. She rushed over to us for a hug.

She had arrived.

We ate lunch at my sister's place, who lived close to the airport. Brianna was able to get a much needed nap and spent the evening walking around downtown Salt Lake City, which was beautifully lit up for the Christmas season.

We finished our evening off at my uncle's house to get some sleep before heading back to Idaho in the morning. Everything was running pretty smoothly, considering that the whole situation was rather overwhelming for Jammie and me, and especially for Brianna. She handled it much better than I would have when I was fifteen.

Brianna's arrival to Utah changed a lot of things back home in Mississippi. She had been worried that her complicated situation would become even more complicated the more others found out, so she asked her mother and siblings not to tell her father, who lived on the other side of town, or the rest of their extended family until she made it out west with us.

About the time we were sitting down to dinner at my uncle's place in Salt Lake City, Brianna's mom was on the phone with Brianna's dad telling him where she was, and about her adoption plans.

I awoke that next morning on an air mattress in my uncle's living room to the sound of Jammie's cell phone. I did not recognize the out-of-state number and I had to wonder who would be calling at such an early hour. It was Brianna's mother calling, and she was frantic. She had been trying to call Brianna's cell phone, but it was turned off.

After Brianna's father heard the news the day before, he spent all evening thinking about how he could get Brianna back home. He hated the idea of his daughter being on the other side of the country with a bunch of strangers at such a time. He wanted her home immediately.

We did not know Brianna's dad. We had never talked to him or exchanged e-mails. We did not know how he would react. The only thing we knew was that Brianna was worried he would not be on board with the idea, and she was worried he might try to stop her. She was right.

I felt bad for him. I could not help but wonder if I would react just the same if I were in his shoes.

While Jammie and I were downstairs in my uncle's kitchen nervously eating cereal, Brianna was upstairs talking to various people on the phone about why she was making these decisions. We were not part of any of those phone conversations. We did not know if her dad would successfully talk her out of the decision she had made. We did not know if her father would show up at our doorstep the next day demanding she come home. Everything was up in the air. We could only worry, wait, and hope.

Normally, the more I think about something out of my control, the more anxious and worried I get. That was not the case that day though. As nervous as I was, I still felt a sense of peace. It was as if a voice inside was telling me that it had been a miracle to have made it this far in our story, and it was not all going to have been for naught. My rational brain was trying to tell me this new dilemma was at least as serious as anything else we had faced, but my heart was telling me it would all work out. I did not know how, but I knew somehow it would happen.

About the time we stopped for lunch along the interstate to Boise, Brianna's siblings sat down to lunch with their dad to discuss Brianna's situation. They were all on Brianna's side, and while I do not think the talk over lunch changed his mind, it did soften his heart.

About the time we sat down for dinner back home in Idaho, Brianna's dad was having a heart-to-heart talk with his sister about a time she found herself in a similar situation. Brianna's aunt had become pregnant at a very young age, and she raised her baby as a single teenaged mother. While she very much loved the child she had raised, she shared with him some of the struggles that Brianna would have to face if she raised this child on her own. Her opinion was that if adoption was what Brianna wanted, he should not stand in the way.

Brianna's siblings and aunt were a strong force in favor of the adoption, but they were not the only ones weighing in on the situation. Other relatives were very much against the idea and they made sure her father knew it. Brianna's aunt and uncle felt very strongly that the baby should stay in the family and they insisted they be allowed to raise it, but Brianna had already considered them and decided against the idea.

When Brianna's father called her the next day, his words were a wonderful surprise. He had spent the entire night searching his thoughts. He had come to the conclusion that he was willing to accept Brianna's decision. Actually, he was not only willing to accept it, but he decided from that point on that he was going to be a support. He was as good as his word. From that day forward he stood behind her. He gave all of the love and support a man could give his daughter from so far away.

It was even better than we could have hoped for. We felt optimistic, like things were now going to continue on track. Everything would have been much more difficult for Brianna without the support he gave from that point on—especially now that Brianna was a pregnant teenager in a strange home and without any local friends.

1-6

AN INTERESTING SOLUTION

When Brianna had first contacted us months earlier, we told everyone the news that a baby could possibly be coming our way. Jammie and I had shared updates with people everywhere we went. At that time, we had never expected any of our friends to ever meet Brianna. When we found out Brianna was coming to Idaho, we worried she might feel uncomfortable knowing that so many strangers knew so much about her. We worried that every eye at church would follow her as people stared and whispered. People tend to do that no matter what church or social group they belong to. It is human nature.

Since Brianna showed interest in going to church with us, we shared with her these concerns and asked if she would prefer we attend somewhere else for the time being. We quickly realized that we were much more worried about it than she was. We drove the point home that people may do something to make her uncomfortable, but she insisted it was not going to be a big deal. Besides, the plan was for her to be with us in our home for only a week anyway, just until after Christmas, and then she would stay with someone else for a few months until it was time to return to Mississippi.

Once Brianna was with us in our home, there were a lot of things that needed to be taken care of. Brianna needed help setting up some doctor appointments. Brianna was still a minor, and because a lot of medical things (as well as other things) could go wrong, and her parents would not be there to sign, it was best that we got a lawyer to draw up some paperwork for us to have temporary guardianship. Brianna also needed to meet with her new caseworker at least once every week. She was able to attend a support group once a week for birthmothers, expecting mothers and single mothers. Jammie took care of the majority of these appointments along with many other things Brianna needed accomplish.

Jammie was all over the place with all of the aspects of the adoption as well as caring for a teenager. Many of the things that needed to be done had to be taken care of while I was at work, so I was not usually able to help. Other than a few things here and there, my schedule carried on pretty much like always. Jammie was the one who had a whole new busy schedule.

Our plan for Brianna to stay in our home for just a week got stretched to two weeks, then to three weeks, then longer. We had more than one generous family express a willingness to let her stay with them, but with all of the new responsibilities on Jammie's shoulders and the busy schedule, it just became easier for Brianna to stay under our roof. Plus, we had always considered it an option to have her stay with us the entire time, but we did not want that to be our primary plan in case something went wrong or was too uncomfortable.

It was hard to predict how things might go with a guest for two months, especially when the guest was almost a complete stranger. Things were going well though. Considering she was only fifteen, had no local friends her age, was pregnant, did not have a whole lot of enjoyable things to occupy her time during the day, had the hormones of pregnancy, and was far away from her family, she seemed to be doing rather well with the situation. Sure, some days were tougher on her than others, but she was a real trooper. She responded well above the age level of what I would expect from a typical fifteen-year-old.

Our caseworker, Jon, wanted to make sure everything with our situation was done by the book. He wanted to make sure Daren had the ability to choose to parent this child if he wanted to, and wanted to make sure our situation could not appear like we were hiding Brianna or the baby from him.

We had heard stories about birthmothers who had gone to other states in order to hide from the biological father, often lying to him about the situation until after the adoption was finalized. We did not want our situation to appear like that. We did not want to lie to Daren. We did not want to cheat him out of a chance to raise his son if that was what he wanted to do.

Jon asked Brianna to start some correspondence with Daren in order to create a paper trail to prove everything had been done legally and honestly. She began by writing him a simple letter, telling him where she was and what she was doing. This information was not going to be new to him. He already knew she was with us in Idaho, but we felt it was important to have it on record. She sent it via certified mail in order to have proof that he received it. After some time passed and he did not respond, she sent him a text message asking if he got it, and he replied that he had.

Over the course of a week, Brianna and Daren exchanged text messages, all of which we kept for our records. Their new correspondence seemed to have rekindled in Daren a desire to be together again. Much like he had done while she was still back home, he rarely mentioned her pregnancy or the baby, and when he did, he it was done so only as leverage to say he thought they should get back together. When she refused, he began again to call her names and turned nasty toward her. Their correspondence ended when he told her wished she would just go away and not contact him anymore.

Jammie and I knew very little about Daren, and the only things we did know were not flattering—the way he treated her during that week of correspondence, his legal troubles with drugs and school, and so forth. Even though he was not interested in raising this child, we still planned to keep him as part of our open adoption if that was what he wanted. We were not likely going to invite him to our home, but we told him we would be happy to send him updates and pictures.

***

We found a lot of joy in having Brianna in our home. It was fun to really get to know her, and it was fun for her to get to know us. I can only imagine how an expecting mother would constantly wonder if she was choosing the right family for her baby. Any hopeful adoptive couple can make a beautiful online profile and include a bunch of flattering pictures, but actually getting to know the adoptive couple as well as she got to know us was something few expecting mothers get to experience.

The relationship between biological parents and adoptive parents is not a natural one. It is not instilled in us as human beings to naturally want to share the idea of parenthood with someone else. Since we were not giving birth to this child, it could have felt natural to feel a sense of competition for the title of "parents."

We had a lot of emotional and difficult times coming our way, and getting to know Brianna on such a personal level in our home helped us see her as the beautiful girl that she was rather than as competition. She was someone we truly came to love, and not just because she was giving us the gift of parenthood, but because we knew her as a person and loved her as our own. The pull for us to compete with her was always overshadowed by our love for her. We will always be grateful for that.

1-7

BECOMING REAL

One of my friends adopted a son a few years earlier. He flew all the way out to St. Louis to bring the new baby home, but the biological mother changed her mind after the child was born. He and his wife flew home empty-handed. He cried for two weeks straight before they got a surprise phone call from their caseworker telling them the biological mother reversed her decision and the baby would be coming to their home after all.

I think it was partly because of his story and others like it that I was afraid of becoming completely invested emotionally only to be heartbroken if our adoption fell through. With each hoop we jumped through, every new experience with Brianna during her pregnancy, every day that passed and we came closer to her due date, I felt a bit more invested. Still, I reserved a part of myself in order to avoid total heartbreak. I, like many people, have had my heart broken after committing myself to a relationship, and the trauma from those instances caused me to keep myself more guarded when entering new relationships.

With this in mind, there was one thing that I had wanted to do ever since Brianna showed up in our home, and it took me a few days to build up the courage. One evening, while Jammie and I were watching a movie with Brianna, I noticed she had her hand on her belly to feel the baby kick. That was what I wanted to try. After asking her permission, I held my hand on her stomach for a moment, just long enough to feel a few kicks. I wondered if the experience would lock me in to "fully invested" mode with my emotions, but it did not. Maybe it was because I was uncomfortable touching the belly of a woman who was not my wife. Still, even though I felt fairly confident the adoption would go through, I still subconsciously felt the need to keep my heart reserved.

I have heard a lot of people say that the moment it became real for them was when they heard the heartbeat for the first time. I went with Brianna and Jammie to one of her doctor appointments, and I heard that heartbeat. Still, even though I could see in the ultrasound that there was a baby in her belly, and I heard the little heart beating in that baby's chest, it still had not completely become real to me. I was still only *mostly* invested, not completely.

In the early days after Brianna contacted us, long before she came to Idaho, she had grown fond of the name Aiden James. James was the name of one of her relatives and Aiden was simply a name she liked. One day, as Jammie and I were talking, we decided to ask her if she would mind if we changed the middle name. We had grown accustomed to calling the baby Aiden, and we liked the name, but we also liked the idea of getting to be part of naming the child. We were nervous about asking her, but she said she was happy to go along with a change. For the time being, we decided on the middle name of Bryan, being that it is my father's name, and it was also similar to Brianna's name.

I was excited about that change. Still, it was only a day or two later that Jammie and I asked her if we could change the first name also. Her reaction was the same—she was happy to let us change it. Even though we were changing the name from what she had chosen, we had not yet picked out a new one. We wanted to do that together with her. We spent hours that evening making lists and comparing them.

My middle name is Ira. I got the name from my grandpa whom I admire and adore. Even though I had wanted to name my son Ira ever since I was a kid, I grew up thinking that my wife would not likely want to go along with it since it is such an uncommon name. Jammie had always told me she liked it, but I always wondered if she would change her mind when it actually came time to pick one. I thought it was even less likely that Brianna would like it, but after a few hours and after considering a few hundred names, the name Ira ended being chosen. I was surprised and elated.

Since the first name came from the top of my list, we thought it could be fun to choose the middle name from the top names on Brianna's list. Much to our surprise, the name

Porter was one of her favorite names. That name was high on all three of our lists. That was my great grandfather's name. That decision came pretty easily.

It is hard for me to explain why, but naming the child was a very big moment for me. Feeling the baby kick was nice, but it did not change much. Hearing the heartbeat and seeing the ultrasound was also nice, but it did not change a whole lot in me either. I found the line where, upon crossing it, I was fully invested. All my chips were in. There was no going back. If something went wrong in the process and this baby to be named Ira never came home with us, I would be utterly heartbroken. My defenses were now down.

Even though Brianna was committed to the adoption, and we were fully invested as well, the fact that we were sharing a home made it difficult to fully prepare ourselves for what was about to take place. We were on the receiving end of the adoption, and she was on the giving end. On the surface, it sounds like such a rosy and happy thing to think about, but it was not easy. We felt an incredible amount of guilt along with our joy. It was hard to not feel guilty for our happiness when someone else was going to have to suffer so much loss in order for us to get what we wanted—parenthood.

With every adoption, the expecting mother has to prepare for the difficulty of the great sacrifice she is about to make. It is physiologically and psychologically programmed into a woman's instincts to be difficult to say goodbye to her child, even if she knows it is the right thing to do. How was Brianna supposed to prepare herself for that? She did not know many people in Idaho other than us, and we were the ones on the other end of her difficult circumstance. Even though we loved her and she loved us, it was nearly impossible for us, the people she lived with, to be able to help her prepare for that sacrifice.

Also, Jammie and I needed to begin preparing our home for the baby's arrival. We needed things like baby clothes, a car seat, a baby swing and a crib. We wanted to prepare the baby's room for the new arrival, but the room that would become the nursery was being occupied by the young lady who was going to give birth to that baby.

We held off with as many of those preparations as possible in order to spare her feelings, but some preparations needed to be done sooner than later, and we had to do them right there in front of her. Whether the feelings were truly hers or whether they were just in our imagination, we felt guilty every time we sorted new baby clothes or bought home something new for the baby.

For all of the same reasons, we tried to keep our outward excitement to a minimum. We knew she wanted us to be excited, and we knew that she knew we were excited. Still, we felt guilty if we showed that too much in front of her, like we were rubbing it in her face.

Since we needed a little bit of time to prepare, and because she could use some space in order to prepare her heart for the separation, we discussed some new options with Brianna. We decided together on a day that she would begin staying with someone else. We felt that one week before her due date would be a good idea. This was a hard decision for us since we had grown accustomed to having her in our home. We also felt responsible for her. We were obviously invested and interested in every detail of her life. We enjoyed her company. We felt guilty for having her leave our home—like we were kicking her out—but we really needed the time to prepare emotionally and temporally.

The main reason we chose that time for her to stay with someone else was because that was when her mother would be arriving in Idaho to support her. She would not have to be left living alone with strangers.

We had a few options as to where the two of them could stay, and we let Brianna meet the families so she could choose. She chose Luke and Jill, some of our best friends who lived only a few blocks away. We made all of the preparations for Brianna and her mom to stay there. We thought we were all set.

Not many days before her mom arrived, however, Brianna expressed concern about how hard it would be to stay with Luke and Jill. They had three boys under the age of five, and being around that all day would be too much for her while trying to cope with her loss. All of the other families who had expressed a willingness to have them in their homes were in similar situations. Most of our close friends were our age, which meant that most of them had babies and toddlers.

Jammie and I drew up a new list of friends we trusted with a situation so delicate. This was a lot to ask of someone, and it was not easy to find a home with just a few days' notice. David and Joyce were friends from church who, after asking them if they could help, told us they needed to give it some thought. They ultimately agreed to take them in. They were exactly whom we were looking for since their kids were all grown up and moved out of the house. They had an available room in their house, and, above all, we trusted and admired them.

There was still a problem with the situation, though. David and Joyce were not going to be available to house them the entire time. Their spare room was only available *after* the baby was born, but not during the week prior to her due date.

Just two days before Brianna's mom was to arrive, we got a call from another friend, Marilyn, who told us she overheard Jammie and Joyce talking about our predicament at church. She and her husband, Joe, stepped into the role that we so desperately needed filled. Like David and Joyce, their children were all out of the home and they had a room. And also just like David and Joyce, we admired and trusted them fully.

We were all set.

When Brianna had hopped onto a plane a few months earlier, we had been worried about her flying standby and getting stuck in a strange airport somewhere. When it was her mother's turn to fly out west, we found that those worries had been justified. Her mother's flight plan was to make a few connection flights, ultimately arriving all the way to us at the Boise airport. She had a nightmare of a time trying to get her

63

seats on each connecting flight, and we were left in the dark wondering when she would arrive. She finally landed late at night, much later than we had originally expected her to arrive, but her luggage did not. It took a lot of work to sort it all out.

We dropped Brianna and her mother off at Joe and Marilyn's house before driving home. For the last time until some future day when our children would be grown up and gone, we were alone in our home with just our dogs to keep us company.

We had a lot to do to get ready during that week. Most of our needed preparations were mental. When Jammie and I needed a break, felt cooped up, or needed to talk about something, we took a walk together. We spent a lot of time over that last month wearing out the sidewalks around our neighborhood. Our walks became even more frequent the closer we came to the due date. We had a hard time talking about anything other than the upcoming adoption. In fact, on some of our walks we would tell ourselves that we were not allowed to talk about adoption, and we needed to find a different topic because of how much it consumed us.

Before Brianna's mother arrived to town, we were scared that the baby might be born before she came. Nobody wanted that to happen. Some Braxton Hicks contractions had us worried more than once that it might happen. Because her mom would have to get back to Mississippi for work, we also did not want Brianna to go past her due date. She had an appointment at 11:00 A.M. to be induced on her due date to ensure enough time to physically heal and be ready to return home when her mom needed to go back.

Jammie and I both had an impossible night's sleep ahead of us the night before her appointment. We made a weak attempt to go to bed early that night, knowing that we were in for a long day once we woke up. At 3:30 A.M., about two hours after I did finally fall asleep, my phone rang. The call was coming from Joe and Marilyn's house. It was time to wake up. It was time to jump in the car. It was time to pick them up. Brianna had gone into labor on her own a few hours before she was scheduled to be induced. It was time to drive to the hospital. It was time. It was time. It was time.

1-8

THE ROLLER COASTER RIDE

I had been to hospitals when some of my friends and family were having babies, but I had never been there for the whole show. I had always shown up near the end, waiting in the lobby or arriving after the baby was already born. Brianna was generous enough to let us be a part of her big day. Her mom was her most important supporter throughout the process, but we got to be the secondary comfort. She allowed us to be there in her room the entire time.

Jammie and I will never be able to thank Brianna enough for this. It would have been completely understandable, and we would have never dreamed of trying to change her mind if she preferred not to have us there. That time at the hospital belonged to her. The hospital room was hers. The day was hers. She chose to share it all with us.

She progressed quickly at first, which made me think the baby was coming right away. We had been looking forward to that moment for months, but now that it had arrived, I struggled to enjoy the moment because I was so tired. Back when I was a single college student, I used to work one or two graveyard shifts a week. With a few more years under my belt and a wedding ring on my finger, I had become accustomed to a steady sleeping schedule. I had become an incredible sissy when it came to losing sleep. Two hours of restless sleep was not enough.

I sat in my chair by Brianna's bedside trying to keep my eyes open while everyone else fulfilled their duties. I was relieved when the nurse gave her something to help with the pain, which slowed her labor down and eased her pains enough that Brianna fell asleep. The excitement mellowed, and about the time the sun came up, I was able to recline in my chair and take a nap. I slept for only about half an hour, but when I woke up I was a new man. I was ready.

Before that day, Jammie and I still hadn't had any direct contact with Brianna's father. We did not know how emotionally attached he was to the situation, but that became clear as the day unfolded. With Brianna obviously busy and distracted, Jammie kept him up-to-date with Brianna's progress. Text messages streamed constantly between their cell phones. His text responses were so quick that we pictured him pacing all morning with his phone in hand, waiting for every update. He sent a delivery man every few hours with flowers and other fun gifts to show he wished he could have been there. His presence and love were felt throughout the entire hospital experience, and it helped start a fun relationship with him that we have enjoyed ever since.

When time came for the big moment, everyone took their positions. Jammie and Brianna's mom stood on either side of the bed to give her emotional support. The doctor and the nurses stationed themselves at the foot of the bed for physical support. And I stood out of the way where I could cheer everyone else on.

Brianna was amazingly calm considering she had been in labor for over ten hours, and was delivering a baby for the first time. Jammie and Brianna stayed perfectly calm as well. I did my best to follow suit, but it did not take me long before I knew I would be wise to pull up a chair rather try to remain standing. The intensity of the situation was beginning to overwhelm me and I was starting to feel light-headed. My vision became cloudy as I came close to passing out, but I never did quite lose consciousness. I doubt Jammie will ever stop teasing me about that.

At about ten minutes before two o'clock in the afternoon, Brianna gave birth. As soon as I saw the tiny baby, I immediately looked wide-eyed at the doctor and nurses to see if their faces would show any alarm. I had seen babies that were a few minutes old before, but never one right when it was born, and I didn't know if a newborn was supposed to look like that. Everyone from the hospital staff appeared excited, so I breathed a sigh of relief knowing all was well.

The nurse handed me the scissors, and I tackled my only delivery room responsibility by cutting the cord.

The most beautiful little boy I had ever seen made his debut into our world. That's right—we now knew for sure that he was a boy.

Happy birthday to Ira Porter Elkins.

Ira, who happened to be born nine months after Jammie and I had first entered the adoption agency, was now part of our crazy world.

Jammie and I stood together, hand-in-hand, as we watched the nurses clean Ira up. When Jammie called out his name for the first time, he stopped crying for a moment and turned his head toward her. Many people might say it was just a coincidence, but it is much more fun to think it was not.

Something else interesting happened that day. My grandfather, the same grandpa who had the name Ira before me, was living in hospice care in another state at that time. On the same morning Ira was born, they hospice staff could not wake him up. The orderlies knew he was still alive, and they tried all of their normal tricks to awaken him, but he never did the entire day. The next day he woke up and, as if nothing out of the ordinary had happened, told the orderly he was hungry.

I like to think Granddad was there in our hospital room with us that day. He will always be someone very special to me, and I like to think he got to take a short vacation from his

70

frail body—even if it was just for a day—to come spend some time with us. I like to think that the love of his life, my grandmother, who had passed away a few years before, came to take him on his little vacation and that they got to watch the whole thing unfold from the other side. I like to think it was not a coincidence that the day he did not wake up was the same day his great grandson, who received his name, was born.

As I said before, the stay at the hospital belonged to Brianna. We, ourselves, were guests there. This baby was not ours. He was still Brianna's baby. Although the hospital gave Jammie and me our own room separate from Brianna's, it was still Brianna's situation. It was hard for some of our friends to understand, but we did not feel like it was our place to invite a lot of friends and family to come share in the joy. Plus, it was a deeply emotional time for everyone, and it was nice to share it mainly with just Brianna and her mom.

That being said, with Brianna's approval, we did invite a select few to come visit the hospital. My mother was in town to help out with anything we might need as well as help with my brother's family since they were expecting a baby on the same day. My sister-in-law, Beth, did not go into labor that day, so she and Clark came with my mom to see us. We knew their kids were excited to meet their new cousin, but the time was not right, and we asked them to wait until Ira could come home with us before meeting him.

71

Although Ira spent the majority of that afternoon and evening with us in our room, we knew it was always Brianna's right to see Ira whenever she wished. If she asked for him, we did not hesitate to bring him to her. It was not easy. We fell in love with him from the first second we laid our eyes on him, and we were terrified something might happen to take Ira away from us. Mainly, we were scared about their bonding time. We were scared she might bond too closely to him, and she would not be able to put her signature on the release papers. We were afraid her emotions might take over, and she would not be able to let him go.

Jammie felt a strong impression to ask Brianna if she wanted to spend some time with Ira before going to bed that first night, and Brianna said she would. We brought little Ira into her room, and left them alone. We told her to let us know when she wanted us to come back since the plan was for him to spend the night with us in our room.

We did not set a time for our return to her room, so we did not know how long she would want to spend with him. Judging by how long she chose to hold him throughout the day, we expected her to want to snuggle him for ten or fifteen minutes.

We waited.

Fifteen minutes passed and we still had not heard from them. We tried to find something on TV worth watching, but nothing could take our minds off the situation, so we just turned it off.

Thirty minutes passed. I have a hard time sitting still when I am nervous, so I paced around the floor. What was going on in the other room?

Forty-five minutes passed and our minds started racing through different scenarios of what they might be thinking or doing in their room. Why had she not called for us to come pick him up?

Sixty minutes passed and we were starting to go out of our minds. Was something the matter? How closely were they bonding? We got out some playing cards and began playing the slowest game of SKIP-BO in history. Was she going to keep Ira all night?

Seventy-five minutes passed and time felt like it was moving as slowly as our card game. What frame of mind was Brianna in? Was she going to be able to sign the custody papers in the morning?

Ninety minutes passed and we just could not handle the suspense anymore. Even if she told us she needed more time, we just had to know. Our minds felt flooded with possibilities and we were drowning.

We knocked softly, and poked our heads into her room. The first thing we saw was Brianna's red puffy eyes. She had been crying. We did not know what to say or what to ask, but once we started talking, it did not take long before we were reassured that everything was okay. The issue that had made her cry had nothing to do with Ira or adoption. She and her mom were working through something completely separate.

They had been caught up in conversation, not realizing how scared we were in the other room. We shared some hugs with them before retiring to our room for the night with Ira. We left on a happy note. What a relief!

Jammie took care of Ira most of the night. We had agreed to take turns waking up to feed Ira, but she let me sleep through most of my turns until she was finally too tired.

As long as Brianna needed to stay in the hospital for her recovery, Ira needed to stay there too, even though he was usually with us down the hall. Since we had some extra time, we thought it could be fun to make the best of it by having a birthday party. We asked a friend to bring a cake, and Brianna's dad sent another basket of treats, which we ate together with the nurses to celebrate Ira's birthday. Brianna was feeling in good spirits. We still felt nervous when Brianna spent time bonding with Ira, but not as much as the previous day.

The next morning, a little more than 48 hours after we had arrived at the hospital, the hard part came. It was time to leave. Jon, along with the hospital caseworker, spent a lot of time going over the paperwork. We were not present in Brianna's room during any of their conversations, but we knew emotions were more elevated than they had been at any other time. Putting her signature on the line was difficult for her, but that is her story to tell, not mine. Suffice it to say that even though we had a fun evening with her the night before, we were still really nervous about whether or not she would go through with it.

She was strong. She followed through with her plan, even though it was difficult. She signed the papers.

Even with that done, we were still far from everything being final. The papers she signed that morning were only to release temporary custody to the adoption agency. The agency, in turn, assigned us to care for the child. Custody still belonged to Brianna and Daren until the time would come for Brianna to stand in front of a judge, which we expected to take place in about a week. After Brianna's time in front of a judge, it would still take another few months before Jammie and I could finalize everything through the court system.

There were still a lot of hoops to jump through, which kept us scared that something might go wrong. We had Baby Ira with us now, and we were madly in love with him, but we were terrified something might happen to take that away from us.

Those fears would only intensify over the coming weeks as we found ourselves at the mercy of more difficulties.

1-9

FRANTIC FIRST DAYS

Open adoption comes with interesting internal battles that can sometimes take a long time to resolve. Are we parents or are we permanent babysitters? We can easily tell ourselves that we, of course, are parents, but sometimes what we know and the way we feel do not match.

Ira was now in our home, but we still did not have anything signed by a judge declaring us to be parents. Brianna still had legal say over Ira, and temporary custody still belonged to the adoption agency—not to us. Even though we were the ones waking up at all hours of the night to warm up a bottle and change a diaper, we did not have any more legal rights to Ira than any stranger walking down the street. At that time we were still babysitters hoping to become parents, even though we loved him as if he were already our son.

Meanwhile, Brianna and her mom were staying with David and Joyce. We stressed and worried about Brianna. How much was she struggling now that the little boy who had been inside her for the last nine months was now with us a few blocks away? Was she regretting her decision? She was still about a week away from her court appearance. Was she going to change her mind?

All of the stresses and insecurities intensified when she and her mom arrived on our doorstep for a visit the next day. We could see by the look on her face the moment she arrived on our doorstep that she had been struggling mightily. We tried to have a nice visit, but she was full of a million questions and she voiced them all one by one.

What if one of us died? What if both of us died? What if we divorced? Were we going to turn our backs on her now that we had Ira? All of her questions were justified, and all of her concerns were legitimate, but there was not much we could say. Nobody can promise he or she will not die, and people do not get married expecting to divorce. All we could really do was assure her that our marriage was strong, our hobbies and interests were not life-threatening, and we loved her too much to ever cut her off.

The thought of asking anything at all from Brianna at such a delicate time made us uncomfortable, but we felt like we needed to. For our own sake as well as for hers, we needed to plan some sort of schedule so we could know how often to expect visits while they were still in Idaho.

I have felt God's guidance a number of times in my life, but there have been only a few times when I've said something that literally felt like it came from someone else. This was one of those times.

"We are going to let you make that decision yourself, Brianna," I said. "Don't make it here. Not right now. After you go back to David and Joyce's, take a moment to ponder how often you want to come over while you're still in Idaho. The decision is completely yours to make. If you want to visit every day, we'll make that happen. If you don't want to come at all anymore, that's fine too. You can decide how often, and you can decide for how long you want each visit to be. It's up to you."

I was surprised when those words came out of my mouth. I had not previously considered the idea of giving Brianna complete control over visits like this, especially not now that she was such an emotional mess. I had not discussed this with Jammie either, but I knew it was right for our situation as soon as those words came out of my mouth.

Brianna nodded her head in agreement then turned her eyes back to Ira, whom she was holding swaddled in her arms.

"I don't know if I can let you go," Brianna said as she continued to cry. "I don't know if I can. I don't know if I can."

When Brianna left, she was a wreck. We were a wreck. Our emotions were so paper thin that we felt like we were being blown all over the place. We called Jon and we called the lady who ran the support group for birthmothers. They helped calm our nerves whenever we called, but over the next two days our worries were never more than a millimeter from our minds. Was she regretting her decision? Was she going to change her mind? Could she let him go?

Brianna's mother was in an interesting position. She was watching her daughter struggle, and yet she knew she had to leave the final decision up to Brianna. At the same time she made sure to tell us on many occasions that we should not worry. She told us that even though Brianna was going through a really rough time she was confident Brianna was not going to go back on her decision.

When Brianna and her mother were back at David and Joyce's place that evening, they talked over a schedule. They decided to come every other day until they left town. Each visit was going to be an hour long. That seemed like a good plan to us. It felt good to have something for which we could plan.

The next visit was very different from the first. This time, Brianna came through our front door with a huge smile on her face. When she held Ira, she focused more on enjoying his presence rather than dreading the thought of giving him away. Indeed, as we've heard many people in the adoption world say, she seemed to understand better that she was not giving him up, but that she was giving him more.

Before they came, we did not have any reason to think the second visit would be different from the first, so we were really nervous—maybe even more so than before the first visit. Not only did her demeanor make us feel more comfortable this time, but we able to enjoy seeing the two of them together. And when she purposefully referred to Ira as "Russ and Jammie's baby," we could not help but love her even more. I know that may not seem like a lot to some people, but it meant the world to us. It helped us feel legitimate in the role we were playing. Even though we were still legally just babysitters, she made us feel like much more.

A few weeks later, with the gift of hindsight, we were able to fully understand why it was important for Brianna to be allowed to set her own schedule. It helped her feel like she had some say in what was going on. It would have been harder for her to cope with the situation if she was not allowed to have any control. And by waiting until she was back at David and Joyce's place—a neutral environment—she was able to think more with her rational mind, and not just with her emotions. During her subsequent visits, she did not have such a hard time handing Ira back over to us because she knew what time she would be leaving, and when she would be coming back.

Everybody's emotions were still up and down all week. Just the simple fact that we were brand new parents was enough to make our emotions ebb and flow, and adding the drama of our situation made it even more so.

Our questions and concerns about whether or not Brianna would sign the court papers were never completely out of our minds, but our visits were going well, and each time she came to our home we felt more confident that she would sign. By the time her court date came, a week after leaving the hospital, we felt pretty secure.

Jammie and I did not go with Brianna and Jon to court, and neither did Ira. We waited at home by the phone. They brought with them all of the correspondence Brianna had with Daren over the previous months to show he was not interested in being a father, and that she was not hiding or lying about her situation. To my understanding, the judge did not hesitate and Brianna stayed firm in her decision, although I am sure it was not easy for her.

Our phone rang right about the time we were expecting it to, and we knew we had just cleared another hurdle. Brianna's decision to place her baby for adoption was now permanent. Brianna and Daren both had no more legal rights to Ira than any other person walking down the street. Of course, we didn't either. The soonest we could hope for a court date was still a few months away. Now that Brianna's day in court was done, we still had two last things on our to-do list before she and her mom headed back south. The first of those was a photo session.

Jammie, being a photographer, got one of her photographer friends to take the pictures for us in her home studio. We had a lot of fun, and got some great shots despite the fact that Ira was in a wiggly mood. We will cherish those pictures forever.

The second thing on our checklist was to have a sweet sixteen birthday party for her since her birthday fell just before her departure day. We made her wear a funny newspaper hat, which matched one we made for Ira, and sang the birthday song purposefully off tune. She opened some gifts and we ate some cake with the people she grew close to while being with us. We did not expect David to make it to the party since he had to work, but he found a way to come.

Everything appeared to be done—at least for the time being. Brianna's court papers had been filed. We had finished our photo shoot. We had celebrated her sixteenth birthday. She had wrapped up all the loose ends, and when morning came the next day, she was ready to go. It made us feel good to see how much she looked forward to seeing her family and friends back in Mississippi. She had not seen them for over two months, and she missed them all. The most important thing about it was seeing her focus change to what was in front of her rather than stay focused on the baby that she was leaving behind.

With all of these things accomplished, we felt like the next few months would consist of mostly technicalities before we could coast to the finish line to finalize the adoption. Those assumptions were proven to be wrong when Ira's birthfather and his family decided enter into the picture again.

1-10

THE STORM BEFORE THE CALM

Our new life had begun. Sure, we were not legally parents yet, but we were on the home stretch. We still had a lot of growing to do together, but our relationship with Brianna was blossoming. We thought we could just coast to the finish line—where an Idaho state judge would be waiting with her gavel and maybe even a handful of helium-filled balloons. That was not at all how it happened, though.

We decided to contact Daren. It had been a while since he and Brianna had contact, so it seemed like a good time. We wanted him to be included in Ira's life if he wanted to be.

We wrote to him a short e-mail message. We not only told him we were willing to send pictures and information, but we were interested in knowing more about him so we could answer Ira's questions once he was older. We didn't just tell him we were okay with having contact with him—we tried to encourage it. That being said, it was not going to come without any effort on his part. We wanted just two simple things from him. First, as long as Brianna wanted to be left alone, he would have to honor her wish. Second, he had to respond to our e-mail and tell us that he *did* want pictures and updates. We were not going to send pictures and letters without knowing for sure that was what he wanted.

We did not know if he would even respond. And if he did, we did not know if he would write an angry or a nice letter. He did not respond to us by e-mail at all, but he did take that as his cue to contact and pester Brianna some more. That was not the response we were hoping for.

A few more weeks passed, and through the grapevine Brianna found out Daren was taking pictures of Ira off of our Facebook pages. We had not realized someone could do that without our permission, so we quickly figured out how to change our security settings.

Some people might ask why we would block him from access to our pictures, while also offering to send him pictures. It is simple. Ira, just because of the fact that he is adopted, is already going to have enough drama in his life. He does not need any extra. We did not like the idea of someone sidestepping us to have contact with our little boy.

Soon after that, Jammie got two requests from girls who wanted to become her Facebook friends. Many people automatically accept new friend requests even if they do not know who it is from, but not us. Jammie wrote them both back, asking how she knew them. One of them responded, saying she mistook Jammie for someone else. Before the second one could respond, Jammie dug around and discovered that both of them were Daren's cousins.

Jammie wrote the second cousin again, told her that she knew who she was, and asked what she was hoping for by requesting access to her page. She and Jammie exchanged three or four e-mails, all of which showed that she was very understanding of our situation as well as feeling sympathetic to her cousin, Daren. She seemed like a nice person. Her petition to become Jammie's Facebook friend, however, was denied. She understood when Jammie told her we would be happy for her to have pictures, but we wanted Daren to be the key to opening the communication door with his family and friends. She had our e-mail. She knew how we could easily be contacted. And just in case Daren somehow did not get the e-mail we sent before, we asked her to request of him the same two things we contacted him about. Still, Daren gave no response to us, and he continued to bother Brianna.

What happened next terrified us.

Brianna was quietly minding her own business, busily working at her new job in a pizzeria, when someone showed up with court papers. She called us immediately after she got off work, and read us the papers which made it clear that Daren was planning to use the courts to take Ira away from us.

Jammie and I had grown more in love with our little Ira every second of every day. Was all that going to be shattered? Were we going to lose him?

We had not seen this coming, and we were now more terrified than ever before.

If Jon had any minutes left on his cell phone, I am sure we exhausted every last one of them and more between the time we heard about the court summons and the day Brianna was to appear in court. He continued to do his best to assure us we had done everything ethically and legally, but there was no consoling us this time. We were a wreck.

We could not leave the situation alone, wanting updates from Brianna or Jon any chance we could get. It was hard to get information because Brianna and Jon were both getting their information through secondhand or thirdhand sources themselves. Every day dragged on and no news ever brought us comfort.

During all of this, Ira was still in the legal custody of the adoption agency, which was both a negative and a positive. It was negative because we knew my wife and I had no legal rights to this child we loved with all our hearts. It was positive because the agency had an amazing team of lawyers throughout the country who were taking care of the situation. We would have struggled to afford the help of an attorney since this adoption process had already run our bank accounts dry. There was not much we could do other than pray. Boy, we sure did our fair share of praying—as did all of our friends close to us.

We could not figure out why Daren suddenly cared enough to seek custody after so many months of zero interest from him. It would have been much easier for him to make this decision to parent *before* Ira was born, rather than wait until after his rights had already been terminated. I figured he must not have taken Brianna seriously when she told him what her plan was. That was the only thing that made sense to me.

Then we found out that the real reason was because he had never actually told his parents that Brianna was having a baby. They did not even know! Since Brianna and Daren had broken up, he did not bother to tell them otherwise. I do not even know his reasons for doing so, but he somehow kept it a secret from them until Brianna returned to Mississippi and word got to his mom. From the secondhand information we received, it was clear that the driving force behind all the recent activity was Daren's mom, not Daren.

Brianna's court date was marked on our calendar, and we nervously watched the day inch closer and closer. There was no escaping it. It was coming and we were helpless to stop it. The lawyers kept assuring us that we had done everything right.

We bit our fingernails and watched the phone all day until Jon finally called. It was over. It was done. Ira was going to stay in our home. What a relief!

We had been kept mostly in the dark about the details until afterward, but it turned out that the agency's lawyer worked alongside the caseworker to solve the issue outside of court. At the last minute, the wrinkles in the situation were ironed out without Brianna or anyone else needing to set foot in any courtroom.

I breathed a huge sigh of relief that day, but I have never been able to look back on it with a smile. In a perfect world, Daren and Brianna would both be an active part in Ira's open adoption. The dispute only lasted a couple of weeks, but it has always brought me pain to think of battling with Daren over custody.

When I think about it, I see Brianna wanting *us* to raise Ira, and Daren wanting his *mother* to raise him. Neither Brianna nor Daren were ready or interested in raising him, and only they had the right to decide who would do so. Jammie and I had no right to say he belonged to us. Brianna's aunt and uncle who said he should come to them because they were family had no right to him. Daren's mother had no more claim on Ira than anyone other than Daren or Brianna. Since Daren and Brianna would never agree on who should raise Ira, and since he never offered even the tiniest amount of emotional or financial support during her pregnancy, it seemed reasonable to me that Brianna should be the one to make that decision.

Plus, Brianna told us over and over that there was no way she would allow Ira to be raised in that home. If they were to have succeeded in reversing the judge's decision, then Ira would have returned to Brianna's arms, and she would have raised Ira herself. She would have dropped out of school, abandoned her hopes of becoming a nurse, and spent her time at home as a single teenage mother.

Daren and his parents did not pursue the matter any further. All of the really scary stuff went away, but the childish games were still there. We reached out to Daren one more time, now that all of the ugly court stuff was finished, to see if he was interested in our previous offer. His response was pretty much the same, choosing to ignore our e-mail and hassling Brianna some more.

This time he got one of Brianna's closest friends in on it. I do not know if it was Daren's idea or if she did it on her own, but she started taking pictures of Ira from Jammie's Facebook page, and giving them to him. We had been very careful about which Mississippi friends to allow access to our Facebook pages, and since Jammie and this particular friend had bonded over some heart-to-heart conversations, we did not think it would be a problem. We were wrong. With access to Jammie's account, she was copying pictures and giving them to Daren. How frustrating. We had already reached out to him twice directly and once indirectly through his cousin. We felt like we had done everything but show up on his doorstep or talk to his mom just to try to get him to agree, but he kept playing games.

We'd had enough of the drama. We apologized to everyone we had to block from our Facebook accounts, and deleted all of the Mississippi contacts except for Brianna's immediate family. We did not write Daren anymore.

1-11

FINALLY FINAL

There was no way of knowing how long we might have to wait for our own day in court to finalize the adoption. When our lawyer called to tell us something opened up, and asked if we wanted it, we jumped at the chance. It had been a while since one of our "surprises" had been a good one, so this was a nice change. The thought of the adoption being legitimate and final had us bubbling with excitement.

Even though we wanted to shout our excitement to the whole world, we did not need or want the whole world to show up to the courtroom. Court was held on a weekday during work hours, so we only invited a very small handful of people. That was enough for us.

I had not been in a courtroom since I was a teenager who had been caught speeding. I was a little intimidated by the big oak stand, the judge sitting above us, an air of seriousness hanging over everything, and a bunch of fancy courtroom talk. However, we were not worried about a thing. Our attorney could take care of that awkward legal stuff.

The judge talked sternly about the seriousness of what we were about to undertake. She found it important to repeatedly drive home the point that we were not going to be able to return the child if we decided later that parenthood was not our thing.

After a sufficient amount of sober and serious talk, her lips curled up into a smile. She did not bang her gavel, but she simply said, "It is done." Just like that, it was official. Leaving that courtroom did not give us any new responsibilities we did not already have, but we were officially not babysitters anymore. We were parents! Ira was now part of our forever family.

When we got back to our little home I told Jammie I felt like we just ran a marathon. It felt so good to be where we now were, but the whole process was so exhausting that I did not know how long it would take before I could say I was ready to adopt again.

This race was over, but we knew we could not stop moving. This adoption was an open adoption, so we would still have obligations to fulfill for many years to come.

We made a lot of promises to Brianna going into the adoption, and we had every intention of keeping them. We did not really know what we were getting ourselves into when we made those promises. We had taken classes and read about others' experiences, but open adoption is one of those things we could have never truly understood until we lived it. Besides, even if we had lived it before, every adoption is different.

Brianna pulled away from us a little in order to move on with her life. We still talked on the phone and exchanged e-mails, but not as often as before. Oftentimes we were anxious to know how she was doing, but we did not want to pry when she needed space. Even when we were not conversing a lot, adoption still consumed our minds.

Sharing pictures turned out to be a greater responsibility than we had anticipated and it was difficult to know how to go about it. We had not discussed with Brianna how often we would post pictures, supposing we could figure it out as we went along. When we questioned other birthmothers, they each had different ideas about how often we should share them. Some birthmothers made it sound like too many pictures made it hard for them to move on with their life. Other birthmothers made it sound like too few pictures made them feel abandoned. Most birthmothers made it sound like their needs kept changing over time, wanting a lot of photos one month, and then nothing the next.

When we thought about pictures before Ira was born, we thought the main difficulty would be the time it would take to share them. After he was born, however, we discovered that only covered part of the difficulty. Adoption is emotionally consuming. Both before and long after Ira was born, our emotions bounced all over the place. We felt the joy of finally having that perfect little baby in our home, but we also felt the guilt that Brianna was going through something difficult to bring us that joy. It tore us apart to think of her suffering.

Posting pictures did take time, but that was nothing compared to the stress adoption already had on us. Even many months later, we still thought about it all day, every day. Oftentimes we found ourselves just wanting a mental break from having to think about it so much. The stress around posting updates was mostly because it intensified the fixation our minds already had on the subject of adoption—much more than the time it took to do it.

On the other hand, we truly did want to share the pictures with Brianna and her family. We started to form a fun relationship with some of her family members whom we had never met face-to-face. We enjoyed sharing Ira's photos with them, and we loved hearing back from them when they sent comments about the photos. Jammie set up a special blog with a password just for Brianna, separate from our own family blog, so Brianna could check it whenever she wanted.

Another reason pictures and updates proved to be harder than we anticipated was because we did not enjoy feeling as if we were babysitters anymore. Even though we understood and respected Brianna's role in the situation, Ira was our little boy. Having the responsibility of giving someone updates and photos made us feel like we had to check in with her. Feeling like we had to report to someone else made us feel like we were not the ultimate authority when it came to our little Ira. And if we felt like we were not the ultimate authority, did that mean someone else must be the parent? Our rational minds told us that we were indeed parents, but our emotional minds played tug-of-war with those feelings.

Once we started realizing what feelings and emotions accompanied the responsibility of an open adoption, we could somewhat understand why some adoptive parents cut off communication from the birthparents. We could see it, but that did not mean we accepted it. If contact with Brianna got to a point where we decided it was unhealthy for Ira to continue, we would obviously have made serious changes, but we had made her promises and we intended to keep them. Even though the photos and updates weighed heavily on us at times, we loved Brianna. We loved her then and we always will, so even during the times when our emotions were most intense, cutting her off was not an option.

The difficulty we felt with the updates and photos was all on our side. It was all in our own minds. What I mean is, Brianna was not saying or doing things to make us feel like she questioned our role. There were a couple of times when she asked for certain pictures, but she was never overly demanding or needy. When we felt like the situation was keeping us from feeling like we were Ira's parents, it was because we were facing something that we, ourselves, needed to overcome. Brianna was on our side—not against us. And although we knew this, accepting it was still easier said than done.

Finally, when it came to choosing photos, we struggled to know how many and how often were the correct amount. Everybody we knew had an opinion, of course, but they were not part of our situation. Even other adoptive couples and other birthparent could not fully understand our situation because the chemistry between Brianna and us was different than it was for other adoptive families.

97

There were times when we wondered if we were posting too often on the blog. We could tell she was dying to see them, but at the same time we wondered if having them so readily available kept her from being able to progress. We tried hard to read her state of mind, but reading single-line statements on her Facebook page was rarely enough of a window into her mind to really know what to think. We avoided asking ourselves the question, "Is it really our responsibility to know how she's doing?" We felt responsible for her happiness because we were the beneficiaries of what was paining her. We felt responsible for her ability to move on because we felt guilty about wanting to progress ourselves. We felt responsible for her well-being because she sacrificed so much for us. Our rational minds would say that we needed to give her some space so that those people closest to her could help her heal, but our emotional minds still played tug-of-war with it.

Through the passing months we noticed that our ability to heal and progress was paralleled with how we envisioned Brianna's progress. We felt more calm and at ease with our role when we felt like she was happy. We felt more guilty than usual if we thought she was struggling, even when her struggles were not related to adoption. I know it was probably unhealthy to mirror someone else's state like that, but that was how it was for a long time.

1-12

A VISIT FROM A FAMILIAR FACE

We had chosen to open our lives to Brianna so she could watch Ira grow, and also so that Ira could know his biological roots. Having our adoption be so open was not easy, and we never felt that more than while we planned for Brianna's first return visit. She was coming back to Idaho!

On a number of occasions, we tried to make arrangements for her to come, but plans fell through every time. When she first left Idaho to return home, our plan was for her to visit sometime that summer, which would have been about six months later. We were all really excited about it. As the months went by, and as Brianna felt farther and farther away, our excitement changed to worry. We became more protective of our title as "parents," and anything that could jeopardize that title made us uncomfortable. It was probably a good thing our summer visit fell through because I am not so sure we were mentally ready for it yet.

We considered having her come for Thanksgiving, but that fell through. We talked about having her come for Ira's first birthday, but the timing would have been bad for her schooling. The idea of spring break came up but that was soon forgotten as well. We knew we would do it someday, but two thousand miles between us made it difficult for her to just drop by.

Then one day Brianna's sister called us wondering about our Christmas break plans. She was planning a trip to Salt Lake City to visit some friends, and wanted to bring Brianna along as a Christmas gift. She asked if they could make the five hour drive to Boise while they were in the Mountain West area.

The scenario was perfect. All of the previous plans we made, which had all fallen through, were plans made months before the visit would take place, and all those plans included her staying for about a week. With this short notice, being only a couple of weeks away, we did not have as much time to fret and stress. And since their drive to Boise was only going to be a small part of their vacation, they planned on staying for just twenty-four hours. The thought of having them in our home for longer than a day was not something we were necessarily scared of, but we had so many questions surrounding the visit that a shortened stay sounded ideal for the first one.

After Ira was born, and Brianna returned to Mississippi, I had said to Jammie a week later that I missed having her in our home. We had grown accustomed to having her with us, and we loved her as part of our family. Being almost a year later, though, her memory now felt distant. The distance and the time apart added up to uncertainty. We still loved her like we did when she lived in our home, but we were used to having our home to ourselves again. We were nervous about what might transpire when she came back to visit.

How would we feel if she called herself Ira's mom? We did not want a tug-of-war over who could claim parenthood. What if Ira seemed more attached to her than to us while she was around? We did not want to feel unimportant. What if being back in our home stirred up difficult emotions for her? We had struggled with our own feelings of guilt for so long that we worried watching her struggle might set us back. Our minds flooded with questions.

The day came, and she was on her way. We were excited and at the same time very nervous. When their rental car pulled up to our house, we ran out to greet them. She was now back in our home and it did not take long before our fears dissipated.

Not only did she seem aware of our insecurities, but she went out of her way to show us that she sustained us as Ira's parents. In fact, she repeatedly referred to us as such, calling us his mom and dad when she was talking to Ira, which meant more to us than anything else she could have done. She talked about positive things, and she made us feel like she approved of the way we were parenting him. That meant the world to us as well. It helped us relax. It helped us take a step back from our emotions to look at the bigger picture where we saw Brianna just wanting to be allowed to love Ira. She was not trying to take anything away from us, and she did a great job of helping us to see that.

Having her back in our home brought back wonderful feelings that had been hiding behind our insecurities. We had not forgotten about our love for her, but memories were not the same as having her physically present again. Once she was with us, and she showed us that she was not a threat, we found that we were more than willing to let her back into our circle. We were happy to let her hold him. We were happy to let them play together on the floor. We were happy to let them interact. We were happy to let them bond. It was a wonderful feeling to be able to enjoy watching them together.

Their visit was short. Many of our friends knew she was coming, and they all wanted an update afterward. It was fun to say "better than we could have imagined" when telling them the details of how it went.

Some of our friends told us they thought the visit would be a bad idea. Those same friends constantly told us it would be bad for our family if we kept the adoption open, but they were not in our shoes, and they did not understand our situation the way we did. We knew ourselves, and we knew this was right for us. Open adoption can be very intimidating and scary, but we do not wish we had it any other way. We keep our adoption promises because we love the relationship it has built.

A funny thing happened after Brianna left to go home again. Her acceptance and support of our parenthood meant so much to us that everything inside of our hearts regarding adoption relaxed. It changed the way our minds processed the situation. We now look forward to a second visit someday rather than being scared like we were of the first one. Sending her pictures feels different now too. Having confidence that she sustains us helps us feel more like we were *sharing* the pictures rather than feeling like we were *reporting* to someone. In fact, oftentimes when we take some fun pictures, Brianna is the first one we think of and we cannot wait to share them with her.

We have not spent a lot of time talking about it with her, but we have felt things change on her end as well. It has been comforting for us to watch her heal and pull away enough to live her teenage life again. We had not been able to separate our emotions from hers during that first year while she struggled because we mirrored her emotional state, so it was nice to be able to watch her heal. She had already been progressing before the visit, but the visit seemed to serve as a catalyst to push that forward even more.

We make a good partnership—Brianna and us. We strongly feel she made the right decision when she chose us as a couple. I am not boasting that Jammie and I are the most extraordinary couple, but I mean we are good for each other. Brianna is good for us, and we are good for Brianna. We love her, and she loves us. We make a good partnership.

1-13

OPEN ABOUT ADOPTION

With each passing month, Ira became more and more "ours." Of course, we will never forget the sacrifice Brianna made to bring him to us, but the way we looked at him became different. When he was brand new it seemed like every time I held him in my arms I thought about the process of how he came to be there. With time, though, I did not think about those things as much. I just looked at him and saw him for who he was. I saw him as my son.

It is always funny when other people forget he was adopted, especially those closest to us. Even my own mother said once, "Ya know, he doesn't really look like his cousins." Jammie looked at her wondering if she was joking, or if she had actually forgotten for a second that he had a completely different set of genes than any of his cousins. She had forgotten. It was funny, and at the same time it was refreshing. It is nice to feel that other people see him primarily as our son and do not think about the adoption first. Even Brianna's mother said something to us once, forgetting for a second that Ira had come to us through her own daughter. Some things make me laugh no matter how often they happen.

Even when they mean well, people sometimes say things that can really hit a soft spot inside of us. The struggle against feeling like we were Ira's permanent babysitters was probably our greatest hurdle. Since people in the general public do not typically use the same terminology we do, sometimes what they *try* to say does not come out like we want to hear it. For example, many people do not know to use the terms "birthmom" or "biological mother." They only know one word—mom. And since a lot of people met Brianna while she was living with us, it is natural for them to wonder how she is doing. People sometimes ask us how Ira's mom is doing. To us, Jammie is "Mom." Oftentimes I will answer that by saying, "Oh, Jammie is fine," usually for my own humor's sake, and other times I respond by saying "*Brianna,* his birthmother, is doing well," emphasizing her name.

One lady commented on how much Ira loved music, and she said his mom must really enjoy music. That one poked me a little extra hard because, on top of the fact that she referred to Brianna as his mom, it undermined the nurturing part of child development. In my strong opinion, a large part of the reason Ira loves music so much is because I have played the guitar for him almost every day of his life. Plus, Jammie and I sing to him every night as we put him to bed. I am not saying that his nature and genetics do not contribute to who he is, because they certainly do, but it is never fun to have people disregard our role in Ira's life.

Many people really do get it, though. Sure, those who say hurtful or insensitive things stand out in our minds, but the truth is they're in the minority. It can feel like it is more common than it is because hurtful words weigh more than positive words, especially since adoption is so important to us.

I realized one day that I was also not perfect at thinking before I talk. I do not always consider other people when words spill out of my mouth.

I was talking to a good friend and venting some frustration about something someone had said. At that time, he had one daughter and she was not adopted, so I continued talking and talking as if he was not able to relate. He sat quietly and listened to everything I said. When he did finally say something, he spoke as if he could relate. I brushed it off and continued talking. When he commented a second time, I realized and remembered that his daughter is his stepdaughter. I do not know his wife's ex-husband, so I never think of his daughter as his stepdaughter.

My mind never made the connection that he was in a similar situation to us. Actually, if I was in his shoes, I would probably struggle even more because of how his wife's ex-husband would go out of his way to remind him just who the little girl's biological father was. My friend never said anything to make me feel like I was insensitive, but I left the conversation realizing that I need to cut people more slack when they're insensitive.

Sometimes people misunderstandings can be humorous. When we were shopping for a car seat before Ira was born, the sales lady asked us how soon the baby was due. We told her we were expecting him in just three days, and her eyes shot immediately to Jammie's midsection. Jammie and I both have a similar sense of humor, so neither of us explained her lack of a belly until she stewed over it for ten seconds. We got a good laugh out of it. She was probably thinking we might be wise to go get ourselves an ultrasound before we made too many purchases.

After Ira was born, we enjoyed everybody's reaction when they asked how old he was. Women would usually respond by saying they wished their body bounced back as quickly as Jammie's did. Some things are funny every time.

Conversations with strangers almost always started that way. They would ask how old Ira was, and then comment on how quickly Jammie lost her baby weight. Next, the conversation would inevitably slide right into adoption. If we were going out into the public we could count on adding twenty minutes to every trip because adoption almost always comes up. We enjoyed it. There would have been easy ways to avoid the conversation if we wanted to, but we were both so proud of adoption that we never shied away from talking about it.

Our positive view of adoption was the main reason we liked to talk about it so much, but we also wanted to stand as advocates for the cause because we had not known just how much opposition there was to adoption. We met people who spoke out against adoption because they did not feel like adopted children were as loved by their parents as children who were not adopted. Many people feel that children should always be raised by family, never by strangers. Some feel that the *only* responsible thing for an unplanned pregnancy is to get married and raise the child.

Some people see infant adoption as stealing babies. I've even been called an "adoptaraptor," which made me laugh. I'm sorry, but if you're trying to insult me, I am not going to feel bad if you use cutesy words like that. They picture people like us and adoption agencies as those who stalk birthmothers and pressure them into doing something they do not want to do.

The list of reasons people oppose adoption goes on and on, all of which became very apparent to us after we adopted. We now know that the world needs more people speaking up in favor of it.

The trends regarding adoption have changed over the last handful of decades, leading to where we are now with far fewer adoptions than in the past. There are consistently about ten abortions performed for every adoption that takes place in the United States. Grandmothers are more willing now to take custody of their grandchildren. It is more socially acceptable now for teenagers to have babies and become mothers. Being a single mother, no matter her age, is much more common and more accepted in society than in the past. Government welfare programs help support low-income households, which can be a big factor if the father is not there for support.

I, personally, have a real problem with the concept of elective abortion. All of the other trends that I just mentioned, though, are not necessarily a bad thing. I have a lot of friends who are either single parents or grew up in a single-parent home, and their home life is beautiful. Sometimes Grandma is the perfect choice for raising a child. Jammie and I know a lot of teenage mothers who have chosen to raise their babies, and we have no hesitation in saying their decision to parent was right for their situation.

I was shocked when I started to see the pressure that a single mother is put under after others find out she's pregnant. I am not specifically talking about Brianna here, though she did feel it too. There's an incredible amount of pressure from family members for a single mother to keep the baby, sometimes saying that she dug herself into a hole, and the only responsible thing to do would be to take care of it. Other family might pressure her into keeping the baby because they want to be a grandma, or uncle, or whatever. The bottom line is that outside pressures from peripheral people sometimes push an expecting mother into making a decision she might not think is the best for her situation. That goes the other way too. If a young woman feels like she was forced into choosing adoption, there would be a good chance the experience will always haunt her.

Once a young lady has made up her mind to place a child for adoption, the pressures from other people do not disappear. With so many people waiting to adopt, and with so few babies, as soon as word gets out about her situation people often start to swarm her. All of a sudden it seems like everybody who knows her also knows a couple who is waiting to adopt. They tell her that she's an answer to their prayers. They put on their best face and talk about all the wonderful qualities their childless friends have. It is a difficult balance for people on our side of the fence to find since adoptive couples do need to be active in marketing themselves in order to get chosen. Still, I've watched pregnant women squirm at the uncomfortable pressure. It seems to be especially uncomfortable for the women who are still undecided about adoption.

Everybody knows about adoption, but not everybody understands open adoption. If they did, how many people would make a different choice? If they knew that they would not have to say good-bye forever to the child growing inside of them, would they choose something different? If they knew they could change the life of a couple like Jammie and me, would they make a different choice? That is why Jammie and I are standing as tall as we can. We are not out there to tell everybody with an unexpected pregnancy that they should choose adoption, but we are doing our best to help everyone see the new option for open adoption.

Having an open adoption means that we have unique branches on our family tree. Having this unusual family tree means we get to learn new ways to love. We love what open adoption has brought to our home.

Ira is my son. I do not doubt that for a second. I don't care that he doesn't have my genes. It doesn't matter to me if he looks like me or not. Ira is my son. Taking second place only to the day when Jammie and I got married, Ira is the best thing to have ever happened to me, and it was all made possible by a beautiful young mother who was willing to look beyond what she wanted for herself. I know he's my son because I can feel it inside of me. I do not know what it is like to have a biological child, but I do not hesitate to say that I could not possibly love him more if he shared my DNA. I love watching Ira grow. I love watching his personality develop. I love everything about him. I love my son more than he will ever know until he has a child of his own.

OpenAdoption
OpenArms

BOOK TWO of the
GLASS HALF-FULL ADOPTION MEMOIRS series

To my beautiful children.
You make me want to be a better man.

Introduction 2

THE EVOLUTION OF ADOPTION

Jammie and I first decided that we wanted to become parents about six months after we were married, but we did not put forth much effort to make it happen. The only thing we did was decide not to renew her birth control prescription. For a lot of our friends that was all that was needed.

Years went by and we gradually put forth more and more effort. We began to try anything that might help our chances of getting pregnant (even some silly remedies that were based more on superstition than science). I graduated from college and begun my career. We found a new life in Idaho. We made new friends. Everything in our life was progressing except for our goal to become parents.

For financial reasons, as well as our pride, we had been resisting the idea of seeing a fertility specialist. After so many years of failing to have children, though, we had tried everything else. It was time. We tried a variety of treatments, but never saw any positive results.

There were still quite a few fertility treatments we had not utilized, but we had grown weary of trying to build our family that way. We wanted out of the emotional cycle that was forcing us to begin each month hoping our new treatment would work, but which always ended with a negative pregnancy test.

It was disheartening and frustrating to want our own children so badly, and yet to feel so utterly helpless at making that dream become reality.

Adoption had been poking at us in the backs of our minds for a long time, even before we had started to see a fertility specialist. Even though we had been thinking about it, we did not want to take that step until we felt like we were ready for it. As we grew increasingly more frustrated with fertility treatments, we began to fully embrace the possibility of adoption.

We found ourselves smiling when we talked about adoption and gritting our teeth when we discussed more fertility treatments. The idea of adopting was comforting.

It just felt right.

We did not feel like we were being forced to resort to adoption, and that was important to us. We felt like we were making the decision because it was something that we truly wanted. Having children biologically was not as important to us anymore. We were excited about adoption!

Like many people, Jammie and I had quite a few mis-
conceptions about adoption when we first stepped into the
adoption agency. Adoption has been around as long as humans
have, but just as societies have changed over time, adoption has
too.

The twentieth century saw a gradual increase in unwed
pregnancies. During the earlier decades of the century people
had a tendency to want to keep these things hidden from the
public. In the hope of protecting privacy and anonymity, laws
were enacted in the United States that sealed up adoption
records, making them inaccessible to people outside the agency.
This increase in privacy led to higher numbers in adoption, and
as the number of unwed pregnancies continued to increase, so
did the number of adoptions, peaking in 1970.

Abortion was soon legalized and birth control became
much more common, leading to a decrease in children being
born to unwed parents. The 1970s also saw a sharp rise in
government assistance programs for single, young, and lower
income families. Society began to be more accepting of single
parenthood. These things, along with other factors, contribut-
ed to a dramatic decline in the number of adoptions. In 1970
close to 9% of children born to unwed mothers were placed for
adoption. By 1981 that number dropped to about 4%. Since
the early 1990s, that number has not risen above 1%.

During the same period of time that the rate of adoption
declined, the number of couples wanting to adopt increased.
The line of people hoping to adopt grew longer and longer.

121

Also during this time of change, while the number of adoptions was changing, society began to change the way it viewed adoption. The desire for secrecy in adoption was being pushed aside by the increased interest of adopted children who had grown older and now wanted to reconnect with their biological families. The laws regarding adoption records began to change, and the requirement for keeping adoption records private was removed.

An increase in adopted children and biological parents wanting to reconnect led to more change in the thinking that surrounded adoption. People placing children for adoption began to expect that they would be able to keep at least some kind of connection with their biological child from the very beginning of the adoption process. These adoptions are now known as "open adoptions."

The term open adoption means that there is contact between the biological parents and the adoptive family. The amount and type of contact between those involved varies greatly from situation to situation and from state to state.

In the late 1980s, it was estimated that only about 30% of the adoption agencies in the United States even offered the possibility of open adoption. By the mid 1990s, however, that number rose to almost 75%. The agencies that did not offer open adoption struggled to catch the interest of potential birthparents.

Adoption continued to evolve until open adoption was not just commonplace, but it had become the new norm.

Jammie and I knew from the moment we began learning about open adoption that it was right for our family. We felt nervous and vulnerable when contemplating the possibilities of living with such open relationships, but we also felt strongly that it would be best for everyone involved—especially our children.

We expected to grow as individuals throughout the process. Parenthood, whether brought on by adoption or not, can do that. What we did not fully expect was that we would learn entirely new ways to love. We did not fully understand what it would be like to have these special relationships because they are unique to open adoption. These things were just as true when we adopted our second child as they were for the first.

Hooray for adoption!

2-1

OUR FIRST TIME THROUGH

Our first adoption experience contained a lot of drama and was extremely complicated. All of those details are in my book *Open Adoption, Open Heart*. Summing that adventure up in like this does not do it justice, but for those who have not read the first book in this series...

Brianna was five months pregnant and just fifteen years old when she first contacted us. We were lucky. We had only been waiting for four months, which was pretty quick for the agency we were working with.

The situation proved to be complicated, though. Even though Brianna had been giving a lot of thought to the idea and she wholeheartedly wanted to choose adoption, the biological father was not so eager. He did not want to raise the baby himself, mind you, but instead wanted her to drop out of high school so *she* could do it. As a result, the optimism that Jammie and I had so quickly developed upon receiving her letter was just as quickly lost within the fragile nuances of our situation.

The most unique part of our story is what happened next: Brianna decided to come to Idaho to have her baby. She chose to do this because Idaho's adoption laws, where we lived, are different than those of Mississippi, where she lived. Here in Idaho, if the biological father did not want to raise the child, he could not stop her from placing the baby for adoption.

Hoping to avoid traveling during the last few months of her pregnancy, she jumped on a plane two months before her due date. Since there were so many things left to accomplish before our little boy was to make his debut into this world, and because we felt responsible for taking care of Brianna while she was so far away from her parents, she stayed with us in our home during those months.

Having Brianna in our home really helped us get to know our son's birthmother more intimately than most adoptive couples have the opportunity to do, and in turn she got to know us intimately as well. We did not just get to know her personality; we grew to love her like family.

Brianna was a real trooper. Very few fifteen-year olds have to face something as intense as what Brianna went through, but she handled herself very maturely, especially considering that her body was swimming with pregnancy hormones and she had no local friends or family. She was amazing.

On a frigid winter day, our little boy, Ira, took his first breath. The experience brought a flood of emotions for all of us during the forty-eight hours we were within the hospital walls. Brianna, and her mother—who had flown out for the delivery—stayed in one hospital room while Jammie, Ira, and I stayed in another. It was surreal. I could not believe we were so lucky to have become connected to someone as wonderful as Brianna, and to have such a beautiful little boy to call our own.

As time drew near for us to check out of the hospital, we grew increasingly more worried. With every minute that passed we were more and more attached to Ira, but until the adoption could be finalized we had no legal rights as parents. The only thing we could do was to continue to care for him as we grew more and more attached.

After we left the hospital, Brianna and her mother went to stay with some of our friends a few blocks away. Her first night away from Ira was very difficult for her. When they came to visit the following day, as Brianna held Ira close she repeatedly whispered to him, "I don't know if I can let you go." That terrified us.

Brianna hurt. Even though she had already made up her mind to go through with the adoption, the act of actually doing so was very painful. Seeing her hurt so much made our hearts ache for her. While welcoming a child into our home was one of the most wonderful things we ever experienced, we felt guilty being on the receiving end of what was causing her so much pain, especially since we had grown to love her so much.

Brianna stayed in Idaho for a few more weeks to sign some custody papers with a judge, and to physically heal enough to be able to travel home to Mississippi.

Having little Ira in our arms was a life-changing experience. Our world began to revolve around this new little baby. The legal issues were not yet settled, though. We had Ira in our home, but custody still belonged to the adoption agency until a few months later when everything could be finalized.

Months after Brianna had gone home, Daren, the biological father, surprised all of us by serving Brianna with a subpoena. He was petitioning for custody.

We were shocked.

The things we knew about Daren, while limited, were not flattering. He was verbally abusive to her, which we had seen firsthand in the text messages he had sent to her while she had lived with us. He had been in trouble with the law and with drugs.

We later found out the reason for the court papers. Daren was not the driving force behind the sudden change. He was still not interested in raising a child. We had assumed all along that his parents knew he had fathered a child, but that was not the case. He had kept it a secret, and when his mom found out a few months after Ira was born, she decided she wanted to raise him.

The subpoena really shook us up, but it did not amount to much. A caseworker with the adoption agency, along with an attorney, was able to smooth things over without Brianna ever needing to set foot in a Mississippi court room. With these legal issues resolved, though, we found ourselves with some ethical questions. If the biological father wanted custody of his son, could we rightfully keep him from that? In our minds, it came down to being a battle between what Brianna wanted and what Daren wanted.

Neither of them wanted to drop out of high school to raise this child.

Brianna wanted us to raise Ira.

Daren wanted his mother to do so.

It did not matter what Daren's mother wanted. Brianna's aunt and uncle had also insisted they be allowed to raise the child so that he could be kept in the family, but it did not matter what they wanted. It did not matter what we wanted. The only preferences that mattered were those of Brianna and Daren.

The bottom line was that they were never going to see eye-to-eye on who would raise him, so that decision was only ever going to be made by one person. And since Daren had kept himself disconnected through the entire pregnancy— never offering so much as a penny of financial support nor an ounce of emotional support—she made that decision herself.

Although we resisted his efforts for custody, we contacted Daren three times to ask him if he wanted photographs and updates about Ira. He ignored us each time.

Over the next year, we kept steady contact with Brianna. She was able to gradually distance herself from the adoption and move on with her life. When I say she was able to move on, I do not mean she cut off contact or stopped loving Ira. We continued regular contact through letters, pictures, telephone calls, etc. As time went on, even though we had regular contact, the distance between Idaho and Mississippi began to grow appreciably. So when Brianna and her sister bought plane tickets to come visit, we were pretty nervous.

Even though we spent nearly three months together before and after Ira's birth, being in each other's company a year later made us uncomfortable again. We did not know how she would react to seeing Ira or even how she would react to being with Jammie and me again. We wondered if we would feel less like parents with her around.

Our worries were quickly squashed. Brianna went out of her way to make sure we knew she approved of the way we were parenting. She purposefully referred to us as Mom and Dad with Ira, helping make sure we knew she was not going to try to take anything away from us. Knowing she supported us the way she did helped us appreciate her even more, and our bond grew much tighter while she was with us again.

Our adoption of Ira was the best thing that could have happened to us. We originally thought we would become parents the way the majority of our friends have—biologically. Adoption has never felt like a plan B for us, though. It has always felt like the plan that was meant to be.

2-2

ONE STEP BEHIND MY BROTHER

In order to properly convey my experience with our second adoption, I need to first rewind my life back to when I was young—years before I even met my wife, Jammie.

When I was just a boy growing up, my partner in crime was by big brother, Clark. We did everything together, including all the ways two boys could get into trouble. If only one of us ever got caught doing something naughty, Mom and Dad would always lecture us both together because chances were good that the other had either done it also (but without getting caught), or he would have also done it if given the chance.

Clark is only eighteen months older than I am. We had the same interests, the same group of friends, and the same goals in life, so I was always just one step behind him. That was fine with me. I liked where we were going.

After I graduated from high school, I applied to the same university he was attending. Two years after Clark had gotten married, I asked my girlfriend to marry me. Amber and I were college students at the time and had been dating for about a year and a half before we tied the knot.

Clark and his wife, Beth, did not wait very long before they decided to have children. Their first child was born roughly a year after they were married. Amber and I were not planning to have children as quickly as they had, but only about a month after we had gotten married, she told me she might be pregnant. Even though we had no money and school kept us very busy, the prospect of becoming a father excited me.

About the time Amber told me she thought she could be pregnant was also when things started to crumble between us. Things had actually started to fall apart even before our marriage had gotten started, but it took me about a month of naiveté to realize just how much trouble our relationship was in. I had been waking up every morning with a bright smile, excited to see my new bride next to me, while she was battling depression and struggling to find happiness in anything.

As a result, when she told me that she thought she might be pregnant—and I was bouncing off the walls with excitement— the chasm between our levels of optimism broadened even more.

It turned out Amber was not pregnant, so my dream of being a father would have to wait, but the prospect of someday becoming a father had been planted deeper in my mind than it ever had before.

Only a few weeks after she had thought she was pregnant, she called me at work to say we needed to talk. By the tone of her voice I knew something serious was going on in her mind, and I suspected correctly the types of things she needed to get off her chest.

She held my hand as she looked me in the eye and said, "I don't love you like I'm supposed to."

"What does that mean? What do you mean 'like you're supposed to?'"

"Like a wife is supposed to love her husband. I don't love you like that."

"We have only been married for about six weeks," I said. "You're struggling with the adjustment, I know. But we'll figure this out."

She said nothing, but just shook her head and averted her gaze.

We were able to keep it together for a few more weeks, but things were very different than they were before. She struggled to explain it to me because she could not find the words and did not think I could understand. In the end she decided that she needed some time and space to figure things out.

After being married two months, I came home from work to find her packing up the little blue Mazda Protégé.

"I'm sorry for all of this. I just need to go somewhere to sort myself out—something I should have done a long time ago," she said.

"Where are you going?" I asked.

"To my Dad's house in Oregon."

"When will you be back?"

"I don't know." She pulled a folded piece of paper out of her pocked and held it out for me to take. "I wrote you a note. I was going to leave it for you to find, but you came home while I was still... packing."

I slipped the note into my back pocket without opening it. "Don't go. We'll figure this out."

She wrapped her arms around me one last time before grabbing the handle of her suitcase and walking out the door. I stood in front of our living room window with my hands in my pockets as I watched her drive away.

I was all alone.

The road I had been traveling—the one that I thought would keep me a step behind my big brother—was no longer leading me where I wanted to go. Amber and I talked every day on the phone, but she refused to say she loved me and I could not get her to come back. Months later as my birthday drew near, I asked for just one thing: permission to come see her. When she shot that idea down and gave me a gift certificate to the music store instead, I knew it was time to start considering some difficult decisions.

A little more time passed and any hope I had left for us was gone. I knew it was over. Since we had no children or possessions to fight over, we didn't need to involve any attorneys and the divorce was finalized less than a week after filing the paperwork.

Not only was the girl who I had expected to be my eternal companion gone, but the other person who I felt closest to, my big brother, had just moved to Philadelphia for dental school. As soon as I could spare time away from my college classes I hopped on a plane and flew out to visit him in the hope of escaping the reality of my life for a while.

My flight arrived too late in the evening to catch my niece before her bedtime, but I just had to see her. I had missed her immensely. As Clark and I stood over her toddler bed watching her sleep, I said, "You're the luckiest guy in the world." Clark was a poor dental school student without a penny to his name, but in my eyes he was rich. He had everything.

I threw an air mattress onto my niece's bedroom floor and shut my eyes for the night. In the morning, as the sun began to peek through the blinds, I watched her as she started to stir awake. Her eyes widened when she saw me and an enormous grin spread across her face. When I had last seen her she could not even walk, but she ran across the room and jumped into my arms. We sat there for a long time just holding each other.

Months later, when a new semester started, Amber came back to town. Out of 30,000 students attending the university, she seemed to be the only person I bumped into on a regular basis. Conversations were short and cordial at first, but after running into each other so often, our conversations became deeper. On a few occasions we talked late into the night about all the things that had happened over the last year. She was able to open up and share things she had kept inside while we were married. I still did not agree with her choice to leave, but I was finally getting a clearer understanding about why she had.

Spending time together in intimate conversation brought back a lot of the feelings we used to share. I had been spending months trying to reject the feelings I still had for Amber, but having her near me again brought them rushing back. And although I had my family to support me through the divorce, I could not talk to them about what was going on inside me for fear that they might smack me upside the head and tell me I was crazy for even being around her.

I did not know what to do.

I did not know what I wanted.

Plus, I had to figure it all out on my own.

Then one night after one of our long and intimate conversations, I lay on my bed thinking about everything. My mind went in circles for the first few hours, but around four o'clock in the morning I began to see things clearly for the first time in a long time. I lay there the entire night deep in my emotions, deep in thought. When the time came for me to get up and go to class, even though I had not caught a minute of sleep, I got up and went about my day.

It was a very difficult decision to make, but I knew what I wanted. I knew where I wanted to go. It was time to start over completely. Although I continued to bump into Amber everywhere I went on campus, I was finally able to let her go and start closing that chapter of my life for good.

It took me some time before I was even remotely interested in girls, but I eventually started dating again. Then one Sunday in church I noticed a beautiful blonde I had never seen before. Jammie and I felt a connection from the first time I cornered her by the drinking fountain to ask her name. She was exactly who I was looking for and before long I found myself standing nervously in front of her father asking for his blessing to marry her.

These details may not seem like they would directly connect to my adoption experience (which is why none of this made it into the first book), but these aspects of my personal history would very much come into play as we went through the process for a second time.

2-3

READY TO GO

Our agency's policy required Jammie and me to wait one year after our first adoption before we could apply to adopt again. Not long after our little boy, Ira, had finished blowing out that single candle on his birthday cake, we started discussing the possibility of adopting a second time.

We had not been questioning whether or not we ever wanted a second child, but we did have to ask ourselves how long it would take before we felt ready to do it again. Our first adoption was exhausting. Since it is an open adoption, it has an ongoing nature to it, and although the intensity of the situation ebbed over time, we still felt like we were running an endurance race.

Our relationship with Brianna was going well, but it was still evolving. Changes in relationships produce stress.

Ever since the very beginning of our adoption journey, we have had a tendency to obsess about it. Some days it was all we could think or talk about. It was exhausting to perpetually focus on the same thing, even if the end result was something as wonderful as the idea that we could be parents. We felt consumed by the aftermath of Ira's adoption. The inherent complexity of open adoption made our decision to adopt again more difficult than simply deciding whether or not we were ready to have a second child.

I would be lying if I did not say we were worried about how a new open adoption relationship would go. We were fully aware that we did not know everything about open adoption relationships just because we had done it once before. Even if we had done it ten times, every situation would be different. Yes, we felt like we were on the right path and we were succeeding with our first open adoption relationship, but the birthparents in a second adoption would be completely new; the relationships would be different. A lot of the knowledge we had gained from our first experience would carry over to our second adoption, but not all of it.

We came to realize over time just how true that would be.

Open adoption is a good test of faith for everyone involved. Not only were we looking to add an entire birth family to our already unique family tree, but any future birth family would be taking a leap of faith with us as well, adding us to their family tree. Trust and faith would be required to make our situation work—from both sides. We had to let go of our insecurities and have confidence that God would guide all of us on our path.

Jammie and I discussed our situation, and our decision to adopt a second time came about pretty quickly. One of the biggest influences on that decision was our own experience growing up. The children in both of our families were close together in age, and having grown up that way we felt strongly that we wanted the same thing for our own children. Just how close together our children would be was largely out of our hands, since we would have to wait for birthparents to choose us, which pushed us even more to get the ball rolling as soon as possible.

We had a great experience with our adoption agency the first time, so we did not even consider picking a new one. Also, we had already developed a great relationship with Jon, our caseworker from our first adoption, and we were excited to see that he was going to be with us on our second journey as well.

It is funny, in retrospect, how quickly we got through our paperwork. Realistically, we knew it could take a long time—maybe even years—before we were chosen to adopt again. Still, we wanted the paperwork finished as quickly as possible just in case there was someone out there ready to choose us. We did not want laziness or procrastination on our part to be the reason we missed an opportunity to be chosen.

The paperwork was incredibly tedious, just like it had been the first time, but we spent every free minute working on it until it was done. I did as much as I could, but Jammie did a lot more while I was at work than I could in my spare moments. Along with all the paperwork, we had to visit a doctor for our physicals, get background checks, do some interviews with people from the adoption agency, and have our home inspected by a caseworker. Even though we knew what Jon would be looking for with the home study, we still went overboard cleaning every inch of the house spotless, stressing about every tiny thing.

After the mounds of paperwork were done, it was time to choose a profile picture. The profile picture would be the first thing any potential birthparent would see, so we knew how important it was to choose a picture capable of catching someone's attention. We chose to use a picture of us out in the snow. Jammie, being a photographer, is amazing at photo editing, so she turned our picture into a puzzle. She removed a few of the pieces to reveal a yellow background, which was done to catch the eye of anyone browsing the pictures. We wrote a caption saying, "Are you the next piece to our family's puzzle?" We laughed about the cheesiness of the caption, but cheesy also served us well with our first profile when we caught Brianna's eye, so we were not about to stray from our formula.

After creating the right picture, it was time to write our profile letter. We were able to reuse the majority of the profile letter from our first adoption profile. We did have to alter some sections because we were now a family of three. Plus, Jammie was now a stay-at-home mother instead of having to work a full time job like before.

After finishing our online profile, everything was turned in. We were ready to go! And by ready to go, I mean that we were ready to wait and wait and wait until someone chose us.

We stepped into line with about 950 other couples hoping to adopt through the same agency. There were about eighty couples waiting just in Idaho alone, and the amount of adoptions that took place every year with our agency was only a fraction of that. We prepared ourselves to wait for a long time.

Even with our paperwork finished and our profile available online, we still had to finish at least ten hours of education time. We did not stress about those hours too much since we were looking forward to an adoption conference four months away. We figured we would complete our credit hours there. That was what we had done the previous time, and we had loved the experience.

Although the conference would give us more than enough credit hours, we were also interested in a few of the local classes, so we attended them for our own enjoyment and benefit.

In the first local class, I recognized some familiar faces. I made an embarrassing mistake. I asked someone I knew from before if they were back to adopt again. I then realized I had put my foot in my mouth when he hung his head and explained how they were still waiting to adopt for the first time. And they had been waiting since before we began the process our first time around. I ached for them.

Before the class officially began, the facilitator had us all introduce ourselves, and give some background about our choice to adopt. There were a few people in the class who had not been waiting long, and even a few who had already been chosen and were waiting for their child to be born, but a large portion of the class had been waiting for years. One couple in the room, who seemed like amazing people, had been waiting for seven years.

By the time it was our turn to introduce ourselves, we felt a little sheepish. There we were surrounded by couples who had been waiting since before we had even thought about adopting the first time, and we were back for a second time. We told everyone that we had adopted once already and that we had completed our paperwork as soon as we were allowed to because we expected it to take years. Nobody said or did anything to make us feel uncomfortable, but we felt guilty just knowing that so many of them had to wait so long.

The process of being chosen to adopt used to run very differently. In the days before open adoption was common, adoption agencies and caseworkers were in charge of choosing where a child would go. They placed with whomever they thought best, which often meant they placed with those who had been waiting the longest.

Now it is mostly the biological parents who choose.

Even though I could see the frustration in those who had been waiting for so long, I am glad the system has changed. It is hard for me to imagine how it would be to have a third party try to match us with potential birthparents. Brianna chose Jammie and me because she saw something in us that brought her comfort. In choosing us, and choosing to have an open adoption, our lives became intertwined. Jammie and I are not perfect, but we were a perfect match for Brianna. Her decision to choose us helped build the foundation of love that we were able to build on throughout the years to come.

The bond that began when we were first contacted was exactly what we were hoping and praying for again. We knew things would be different, and we would do our best to embrace whatever those differences would be. All we could do was continue with our faith in the process and in God.

That... and wait.

2-4

THE WAITING GAME

An interesting thing happened right after our profile went live online. Jammie missed her period. It was not unusual for it to be a few days later than expected, but after being ten days late we started to wonder.

It sparked some emotions I did not expect. I had already accepted the possibility that we might never have children biologically. Things got easier for me after accepting that. Especially after we adopted Ira, I had already let go of the need for my children to have the same genes as me.

At first my mind resisted the possibility that we were pregnant. Jammie's missed period did not immediately fill me with hope, but just made me start to wonder. I felt like we were getting pulled into the infertility cycle all over again, which had never amounted to anything more than smashing our hopes again and again. It had happened so many times before that I did not want to deal with it anymore.

We had not stressed about our infertility challenges since before Ira was born. We had already stopped listening to others' silly remedies, including the innumerable people who told us we would get pregnant as soon as we started the adoption process (If I had a dollar for every time someone said that to me I could pay off the house). All of those frustrating parts of infertility had been pushed into our past as we were focusing on adoption.

What I wanted was simple: to be a father again. The thought of having children the "normal" way was getting in the way of my goal.

I know that does not make sense, but in my subconscious mind the "normal" way just did not work for us. Any thought of trying to go about it that way would only end in more frustration. Not only that, but I was excited about adopting again. And if we were suddenly able to have biological kids, that would mean we were not going to be adopting at the same time. I felt like we had to choose.

Those tortured feelings were not long-lived.

My rational mind and my emotions had a little boxing match for a couple of days until my emotions finally won. I became excited about a little one running around the house, sharing my DNA, and calling me Dad.

But that was not the way things worked out.

Jammie and I burned through some home pregnancy tests, which all came up negative. We then tried again because the first test sticks were out of date. We tested again because we assumed we were testing at the wrong time of day. We tested yet again because we wondered if we were using the wrong brand. We tested and tested until her period came.

Although my subconscious had resisted the idea at first, I had become excited about the possibility of my wife carrying our baby. When those hopes were dashed, all of those previous feelings of frustration came rushing back. It took me a day or two to flip my mental switch back to where it was regarding adoption.

Do not get me wrong, we never saw adoption as a last resort. Adoption was a choice for us. It was something that was already a part of our lives and we were excited about doing it again—not because we felt it was what we had to do—but because we wanted to.

It was definitely different sitting on the waiting list to adopt the second time. When we had gone through the process the first time, all we really had in our life were our dogs and an empty bedroom next to ours. This time we had little Ira sleeping in the next room and that one little awesome fact made all the difference in the world. We did not know if we would be contacted within a month or if it would take a decade to be selected, but at least we had our little boy to sugar coat the anxiety of the waiting game.

The answer to our question about whether it would take a month or a decade came when Jammie and I were casually lounging around the house on a lazy Sunday afternoon. Jammie's cell phone chimed, alerting her that she had just received an email. When she told me that we had just been contacted by a potential birthmother, I thought for sure she was teasing me.

149

This is what her email said:

Dear Russ and Jammie,

My name is Darcie. I have been working with the adoption agency over the past few months searching for a family for my baby. It has been a long, hard process of trying to find a couple that I feel would be best for my child. Since we have not been introduced, I am not sure where to start or what to say.

But I'll tell you my story so that you can get to know me a little better.

I grew up in Idaho. For the past three years I have been in college, where I met my husband. Our marriage lasted five and a half months, and then we separated. A week after moving out, I discovered I was pregnant.

Despite everything that was going on, I was overjoyed to find that I would soon be a mother. However, after only a few weeks I knew I could not parent alone and I went back to my husband.

We worked through several months of counseling together, but it did not work out and we finalized our divorce a few months ago. He has agreed to surrender his parental rights upon placement for adoption.

I have moved back home with my mother and will stay with her until the baby is born, and until I can fully recover from my divorce.

I have battled the idea of adoption since I got pregnant and it has taken a lot of faith to follow through and do what I know I must. About a month ago I met a potential adoptive couple, and was surprised by how much I liked them. I wanted to continue working with them but I was recently informed by the wife that they have some issues they need to resolve before they adopt a baby.

I am grateful to them though, because it opened my heart to the possibility that I could feel safe enough to trust someone else to give my baby the life she deserves—the life I cannot give her at this moment.

God has been there for me through this experience and I am relying on Him as best I can with this decision.

The second couple I chose wanted to pursue a closed adoption. We were trying to negotiate with them the kind of relationship I could have, both with them and the child, after placement. I have learned, through trying to mentally prepare myself for that kind of restricted contact, that I need an open adoption.

I know that this baby will no longer be my own, but I can in no way forget or immediately move away from this tiny spirit who has been a part of me since before she was conceived. I want to get pictures and share experiences with her parents as she grows. I want to be able to visit and be a friend to her future mother as well as a support. I want to be a part of her life in whatever small way I can.

What I would like for my baby is a home that is filled with love and laughter, to have a loving mother and father who are patient and have a stable relationship, so she will be able to look to them as an example of how a marriage should work. I want her to be taught at a young age how much God loves her so that she will never question it as she grows, as trials come. I want her to learn that she can rely on Him in all things. I want her to have the freedom to choose her likes and dislikes and be herself even if it is a little out of the ordinary for a girl, even if it is restoring old cars or something crazy. I want her to have a father who knows how to prioritize his family over other activities, to have a mother who is kind and willing to be a friend no matter how disappointed she may be in her daughter's choices.

I want her to be loved.

I felt a very strong impression when I looked through your profile that I needed to speak with you. Since I have not met you, I cannot know for sure if you are the right family for my daughter, but I would like to get to know you better. Feel free to email a response to me if you feel that my baby might belong in your family.

Darcie

It had only been about a month since our profile went live online. We had already been contacted. All those couples who had been waiting for years and years were still waiting, and we possibly had a *second* child coming our way, and only within *two years* of putting our papers in the first time!

We read the letter over and over and over again.

Before we wrote her back, though, we had to tell someone. We called my brother, Clark, and then drove over to his place a few minutes away. We were bouncing off the walls with a million different emotions. We had again begun our ride on the intense emotional roller coaster that ebbed and flowed with alternating hope and caution. We could not help but be elated about being contacted, but at the same time we knew it could fall through at any moment.

Though we told Clark and Beth, we decided we would keep the news a secret for a while. That was a decision we had made long before because of how things went with our first adoption. We knew we would feel secure one day and hopeless the next. It had been fun to tell people the first time, especially when the news was good, but it was not fun when news took a turn for the worse. We decided to keep it a secret until we knew it was a sure thing.

Jammie and I responded to Darcie that same day by writing separate letters and then sending them off together. We thought it would be fun for her to get to know both of us individually as well as to see that we were both involved in the adoption process.

Since Darcie had mentioned her recent divorce, I wanted to tell her about mine. I remembered very clearly all the in-securities I had felt surrounding it—feeling judged by others, feeling like I had failed at something important, and so on. I wanted her to know I had been there. Jammie and I talked about it, though, and decided to save that conversation for another time.

We emailed our letters and then began to chew our finger-nails as we waited for a response, but it did not come that day. It did not come the next day either, which made us twice as anxious as the previous day. When Tuesday came around, our anxiety level had reached its peak.

Then our phone rang. It was Darcie's caseworker. Darcie wanted to meet us face-to-face that same day.

2-5

FACE-TO-FACE

We showed up early to our appointment to meet Darcie at the adoption agency. We sat nervously in the office, staring out the window at every car that pulled into the parking lot, wondering if Darcie was driving each and every one of them. We knew her instantly when we saw her walking through the parking lot. To be fair, that was not terribly difficult to do, since her protruding belly gave her away.

Darcie thought it would be uncomfortable to have the caseworker sit in on our conversation, so she asked to be left alone with us. As we sat down with her, we did not know if we would be chatting for ten minutes or ten hours. We also did not know what we were going to talk about, other than the obvious. We decided to just be ourselves, and as a result conversation came easily and naturally.

We talked about what she had been going through with her decision to choose adoption—a conversation that included quite a bit about her divorce. We also discussed our first adoption and our relationship with Ira's birthmom.

Darcie had been through a lot over the last year. She grew attached to the first couple she had chosen to adopt her baby, but they decided they were not yet ready to adopt.

She started to communicate with the second couple without promising to choose them. She did not commit completely to them because she was not 100% sure she was going to choose adoption, and she was not positive their philosophies of adoption would match with her own. When she did make a final decision regarding the second couple, she told them she would need to choose someone who also wanted an open adoption.

It broke our hearts to hear that the second couple had laid a guilt trip on Darcie's shoulders when she broke the news to them. The only other person besides Darcie who had any say in what was going on was Caleb, her ex-husband. This baby was still their baby. Nobody else had any right to lay claim to this child: not that couple, not us, not even Caleb or Darcie's extended family.

Hopeful adoptive couples should never feel entitled to someone else's child, and they should never put extra pressure on potential birthparents, no matter how badly they want to become parents in their own right.

We listened to the hurt in her voice as she recounted her experience. It brought up some interesting questions and emotions.

At what point does that baby completely and solidly belong to the adoptive couple? Obviously, the simple act of being contacted by a birthmother does not entitle the hopeful adoptive couple. Equally as obvious was the fact that, with more than a year gone by since our son's adoption had been finalized, I would fight tooth and nail against anybody who thought about taking our son away from us.

Since I became active in the adoption community, I have seen adoptions go through a gray area in which hopeful adoptive parents feel like the child is already theirs, but legally that is not the case.

We had found ourselves in that gray area during our first adoption, when Brianna was pushing for the adoption to go through and Daren came out of nowhere to fight it. Our journey down the road with Caleb and Darcie would indeed be very different from our first adoption, but we would nevertheless come to find ourselves yet again in that gray area where it was difficult to know where our legal and ethical rights began and ended.

We made it our main focus to assure Darcie that we would support whatever decision she made. Whether or not she chose us, or even if she chose not to place her child for adoption, was not for us to decide or push on her. A pressured relationship would only cause problems.

Getting to know Darcie was a different experience than getting to know Brianna. Brianna lived on the other side of the country, so email and Facebook were our main forms of communication during those first few weeks. We were in contact quite a bit, but the internet is impersonal when compared to a face-to-face meeting.

Even though we had just met Darcie, we were able to get deep into conversation with her. We talked heart-to-heart and shared some tears together. And even though a big part of me wanted to bring up my divorce and assure her we were not among those who would judge her, the window for me to do so never opened. I know that probably sounds weird since we had talked extensively about her divorce, but it just did not happen at this meeting. The caseworker stuck her head into the room after two hours and informed us it was time for her to start locking up the building.

The only people left in the building besides Darcie's caseworker were the birthmothers (and expecting mothers considering adoption) who were attending their weekly support group down the hall. Once a week the people in the support group would come together and discuss what they were going through. Jammie used to attend the group with Brianna before Ira was born, so she had gotten to know many of the birthmothers, as well as the group leader, Virginia.

It was fun to be funneled out into the hallway all at the same time. Darcie had already met with the group before, so it was nice to get a chance to chat together. When Virginia learned about why we three were meeting together, she turned to Darcie and told her how awesome she thought we were.

We were not seeking any endorsements, but to receive one from a person we all admired certainly was not going to hurt.

Our meeting with Darcie gave us plenty to think about. For starters, we knew a little bit more about what we were getting into this time compared to when we adopted the first time. We knew a little bit more about what adoption relationships were like. I think if we had not been through the process once before, we might have focused more on the prospect of adoption than on Darcie herself. Since we had done that, and because we knew that adopting Caleb and Darcie's child would also mean grafting them into our family tree, we were very interested in Darcie as a person. We were obviously interested in the little one growing inside her eight-months-pregnant belly too, but our minds focused on what Darcie would bring to our circle.

That was another thing—her eight-months-pregnant belly. Not only were we surprised to have been contacted within a month of finishing our paperwork, but Darcie was only three weeks away from the day she was scheduled to be induced. When we adopted Ira, we were chosen about halfway through Brianna's pregnancy and we had a long time to worry about all the ups and downs. With Darcie, we were on course to possibly go from paperwork to parenthood in just seven weeks. That would only happen if everything went through, of course, and we were far from certain that it would.

Our meeting left all of us hungry for more interaction. We set a time to meet up again the following week and we decided to do it at our house instead of at the agency office. Before we met Darcie we were hesitant about the idea of a local birthparent having access to the inside of our home, but once we had met Darcie, we were warm to the idea. Besides, having the meeting at our own home would give us the leisure to talk without worrying about the clock running out.

We scrubbed the house spotless and dressed Ira in some cute clothes in anticipation of her arrival. Things went pretty much like they had before, with conversation flowing easily and openly between us. She surprised us with an unexpected question, though. She said she noticed the six year age difference between Jammie and me, and wondered if there was something that had happened to create such a gap.

Of course there was, and the window to talk about my divorce was now open. I knew she of all people would understand, and she did. I do not go through my life looking for ways to bring up my divorce, but it is not something I am ashamed of and it had been weighing on me ever since Darcie had contacted us. I could see how heavy her recent divorce was on her shoulders, and I wanted to tell her she was not alone, that I understood a lot of what she was experiencing. Her question caught me off guard, but in the end it was nice to talk openly about it together.

Darcie also brought up the topic of naming the child. She was pretty sure from the ultrasounds that the baby would be a girl, and she had thought of a couple names she liked, but she wanted us to name her if we were to be the parents.

Ira is a family name that comes from my father's side. It is my middle name, my grandpa's, and a few other relatives along my family line. We liked the idea of choosing another family name, which led us to choose the name Hazel, which is Jammie's mother's name. Darcie was immediately on board with the name, and it was as simple as that.

Like many couples, Jammie and I had changed our minds a thousand times about the name before we got to the decision point, considering names long before we even turned in our paperwork, but by the time Darcie asked us, we had already chosen the one we liked. And since we had enjoyed involving Brianna as a big part of choosing Ira's middle name, we encouraged Darcie to choose a middle name for Hazel. She did not choose one there in that moment, but decided she would give it some thought.

We enjoyed our visit and looked forward to doing it once more the following week, which would be the last full week before she was scheduled to deliver. This time, though, she asked if she could bring her mother along. We loved that idea.

Darcie's mother was not completely on board with the idea of adoption. This was not something new to us since it had come up in conversation numerous times with Darcie. Her mother was not the type of person to demand Darcie do what she was told, though. She understood this was Darcie's decision, but she was also under the impression that adoption would mean she would not be able to have any contact with the child after placement.

Much of the world sees adoption that way—that the only two options are to see the child every day, or to never see her again. We tried to reassure her of our openness, but she thought it unlikely we would actually keep our side of that type of arrangement.

We talked over dinner before Darcie and Jammie went off into the other room to look at something together, leaving her mother and me together at the table.

At first I thought I was being clever by keeping her in conversation so Jammie and Darcie could have some time alone. Jammie is better at deep heart-to-heart conversation than I am, especially with another woman, so I knew it would be good; it was not the first time I had slipped away to let them have that time. After a little while, though, I realized Darcie's mom was doing the same thing with me: keeping me engaged in conversation so Darcie and Jammie could be alone.

Her mother knew Darcie needed to make the decision for herself, but she also wanted to make sure she was making the decision for the right *reasons*. For instance, she offered to support her financially after the baby was born, if she chose to parent the child. I do not think she was trying to pressure her into parenting, I just think she just wanted to make sure Darcie would not regret her decision.

Before she left, Darcie's mom expressed some emotions about how she was grateful we were in the picture. She was gaining a better understanding of what open adoption was like, and she could see how much we loved Darcie. And by the time they drove away, we felt a much greater love and support from her.

We were glad to have been able to meet and start a relationship with Darcie's mom. Many things were going our way, but we still were not sure if Darcie was going to choose adoption. We did not want to pressure her, because we knew she would regret the decision if it was mostly someone else making it for her, but we could feel it: we were starting to get our hopes up. We felt like she would choose us to parent her child if she chose adoption—we just were not sure she would choose adoption.

Even though we were not sure about everything, we finally decided it was time to start spreading the news. We had started to tell the rest of our close family about a week after we had told Clark and Beth, but now we finally started telling the rest. We made sure everybody knew it was not a sure thing, but we wanted our close friends to have a little notice rather than suffer the shock when we simply showed up one day with a baby. When we broke the news to Clark and Beth's kids, their four-year old got really sad. She did not want the adoption to happen because she thought it meant we were going to trade Ira for the new baby, and she really loved him.

Brianna was the first person other than our siblings and parents to get the phone call, and she ran through her house screaming with excitement. She was beside herself with joy, knowing Ira could soon be a big brother.

We did not talk about the process a whole lot on Facebook when we were going through our first adoption. Since we were connected to Brianna on Facebook from the very beginning, we refrained from posting a lot about the details of our adventure. We knew Brianna would be reading most of what we typed. Even when someone knows they are doing the right thing by choosing adoption, it is common to feel pain from the separation. We knew Brianna would be no exception, so we did not want to rub it in by celebrating in front of her.

Because we had the ability to see Darcie face-to-face and did not have the same need to connect with her on social media, we made no attempt connect with her on Facebook at that time. The news spread through our social media networks like fire through desert grass. This time we were able to celebrate with all of our friends and enjoy the interaction.

We knew celebrating a *possible* adoption meant that we might be setting ourselves up for a crash, but we were willing to take that risk.

We did not think we would know for certain until at least a day or two after the child was born. All we could do was hope and pray Darcie would make the right decision for her situation—whatever that decision would be—and to support her in it.

2-6

THE MOMENT ARRIVES

I sat home all morning with my little boy waiting for my phone to ring. Jammie had already gone to the hospital to be with Darcie and her mom for the early stages of labor. I made some weak attempts at getting some work done, but there was no way my mind was ever going to be able to focus. I was not accomplishing anything.

My phone beeped. Jammie had sent me a text.

She was giving me a heads up that Caleb had come to the hospital and was there with them in the delivery room. I had known Caleb was going to come, but I did not expect him to be there for a few more hours. The selfish part of me was hoping he would be too late for the delivery. I do not mean for that to sound cruel or insensitive, but his presence there worried me.

Part of the reason I was uneasy about him was because my divorce had ended with so many "what ifs."

After my ex-wife, Amber, had come back to town to finish school, and we had started spending some time around each other, our situation got much more complicated. I had such a hard time deciding what I wanted and I could only imagine how difficult it would have been if some of that time had been together in a hospital delivery room.

I had been in Caleb's shoes before—sort of. Amber and I never had any children. I did not know if his presence would cause drama between him and Darcie, or drama between all of us. I did not know how he felt about having us there. I did not even know if he embraced the idea of adoption.

On top of all that were our prior experiences with Ira's birthfather. Whenever the name of Ira's birthfather came up, it was only because he was causing problems. My anxiety was not anything Caleb was responsible for, but because of Daren, my mind had an immediate aversion to the thought of a birthfather being in the picture.

So when I got that text message from Jammie telling me Caleb was there at the hospital with them, my discomfort intensified. Everything was already complicated enough.

Jammie's next text told me she had spent the last little while chatting with and getting to know Caleb, and she said she was sure I would like him. It did not surprise me that she would say something like that. She knew I was not looking forward to spending the afternoon around him at the hospital, and her text message did not change the way I felt.

I went back to my feeble attempt at making my morning productive, but I continued to fail miserably at it. Then the long-awaited phone call came.

It was time!

I quickly strapped Ira into his car seat and drove him to a friend's place to spend the day. En route, every car in front of me drove ten miles under the speed limit. Every time I passed one slowpoke I found myself stuck behind another. Jammie called me a few times as I drove to tell me I had better hurry.

I barely made it in time! The doctor was about to have Darcie start pushing.

Jammie, Caleb, and Darcie's mom stood in the room with the nurses and the doctor. I shook Caleb's hand, then we all went around the room and introduced ourselves. I later found out that the doctor made us do these introductions because he had been thinking all morning that Caleb was Jammie's husband, and he was confused who this big new bald guy was in the room.

We did not feel right introducing ourselves as the couple who was going to adopt the baby, because we still did not know if the adoption would take place. Darcie still had not told us whether or not she was going to go through with it, so we just ended up saying that we were there to support them, and that if they chose adoption we would be the couple.

When it was Caleb's turn—he was the last in line to state his name—he said he was "Caleb, the real father."

That simple statement, "the real father," would normally have been a punch to my stomach. As soon as those words came out of his mouth, though, Caleb reacted with discomfort so quickly that I immediately started to take a liking to him.

It was not that I enjoyed his discomfort, but seeing how he reacted to his own words helped me to see, immediately, that he cared about our feelings. He just did not know yet what he was supposed to call himself. As Caleb appeared to search frantically for a better title than "the real father," Darcie sent him a lifeline and said, "biological father." I saw Caleb subsequently mouthing the words to himself as if making mental notes on the terminology so he could avoid running into that problem in the future.

My experience in Darcie's delivery room was quite different from my experience with Brianna. Brianna gave birth at the largest hospital in Boise, while Darcie chose a tiny hospital in a neighboring town. I had been at the hospital for about twelve hours by the time Brianna gave birth, but I popped in less than five minutes before Darcie was told to start pushing.

One thing that was the same for both births, though, was my inability to calm my nerves. Even though I was not watching the actual delivery when Ira was born, I started to become faint almost as soon as Brianna started to push and I had to take a seat to avoid passing out. For some reason, my stubbornness to prove my machismo was taking over my rationale, and I insisted on staying on my feet for Hazel's birth. One of the nurses could see it written on my pale face and suggested I sit down, but I insisted on staying vertical. I do not know why it affects me so much, because I am not scared or squeamish when I see blood. For some reason, just being in the room when a child is being born sucks the strength out of my knees.

I succeeded, though—sort of. Even with the nurse insisting every three minutes that I take a seat before passing out, my rump did not touch a chair until baby Hazel made her debut into the world. The most beautiful baby girl I had ever seen was born that hot summer day in a small town hospital.

The doctor and nurses quickly asked who was going to cut the cord, but that decision had not yet been made. I knew I was one of the candidates for the cutting ceremony, but I felt guilty about being the one to do it. I was not sure whether or not Hazel was ever going to come home with us and I did not want to take that privilege away from someone else if I was going to be little more than a delivery room memory. They considered me and they considered Caleb, but I was happy and relieved when Darcie asked her mom to do the honors. Truthfully, even though I thought it was fun to cut Ira's cord, I felt like having done it once was enough for me.

While everybody oohed, ahhed and marveled at the beauty of the world's newest citizen, I knew I had to find the nearest place to sit down. The climax of the experience proved to be a little too much for me and I was as close as I had ever come to passing out. My stomach started to turn, my eyes started to glaze, and sweat flowed from every pore. Luckily though, as close as I came, I never did completely lose my grip on consciousness. I still had my machismo.

Once my legs had recovered strength enough to stand, Jammie and I made our way over to the place where the nurses were cleaning Hazel up. I stared down at the beautiful baby girl as she cried and I thought about all the possibilities if she were to come home with us.

The nurses were not at all used to a situation involving adoption. Delivery room congratulations were obviously part of their routine, but they did not know exactly how to go about it. It would have been better if they had just saved their congratulations for another moment, but the nurses repeatedly directed their congratulations toward us more than toward Darcie and Caleb. We asked them every time not to because it was making everyone uncomfortable, but they just would not stop.

After they had Hazel all cleaned up, they tried to hand her over to Jammie and me, but Jammie quickly pointed them toward Darcie to make the decision about who would hold her first.

We waited for a short while in the delivery room as Darcie held the freshly swaddled baby in her arms. As tears slid down her cheeks, she stared into her baby's gray newborn eyes. Jammie and I knew what we needed to do, so we quietly excused ourselves from the room, giving them time alone. We went out to wait in the lobby without even touching baby Hazel.

2-7

AN EVENTFUL DAY

The little hospital did not have a waiting room, so Jammie and I sat together holding hands on some chairs in a corner of the lobby. Trying to sort through our thoughts was like trying to take a sip of water from a fire hydrant. So many emotions flooded our minds that it was impossible to organize our brains. We were so over-stimulated that all we could do was sit and rub each other's hands, staring into space.

Along with everything else that complicated our situation, Darcie had been talking about breastfeeding Hazel while still at the hospital. Many people immediately think about the health benefits of receiving the mother's colostrum and milk, but Jammie and I focused more on the personal sides of the decision. Breastfeeding is an intimate bonding time between baby and mother, and Darcie's desire to breastfeed made us think she was leaning toward raising Hazel, not choosing adoption. We did not feel like it was our place to influence her either way so we left that decision up to her and Caleb.

While we sat quietly in our chairs studying the intricacies of the hospital lobby floor, Jammie asked me if I thought the adoption was going to go through. The answer came easily and quickly to my lips because it was something I had been seriously considering for weeks: my answer was no. I did not think it would go through. I had watched Caleb not only stand by Darcie's side, but he had held her hand during the entire delivery. Darcie had told us she was planning to breastfeed, which meant a lot of intimate bonding time. Plus, Darcie would be at the hospital for forty-eight hours with Hazel, and most of that time they would be alone together. There were a lot of factors influencing the situation, so no; I did not believe the adoption would go through. Jammie did not either.

Jammie and I very much wanted another child, but decided at that moment that we had better start coming to terms with the thought that this baby was not going to be our daughter. Besides, even though we had gotten our hopes up, Darcie still had never promised us a thing, one way or another. We had no right to feel entitled to be Hazel's parents. The decision was not ours to make and we knew we needed to be there to support them in whatever decision they made, even if that decision broke our hearts.

With every minute that ticked away on the clock, I grew more and more convinced that I was right. I became certain during our time in the lobby that God was calling us to be part of Caleb and Darcie's support group, but not to be Hazel's parents. That was going to take some mental adjustment.

We sat quietly in our little corner of the lobby for an hour and a half. At an intensely emotional moment like that, ninety minutes felt like time had come to a stand-still. We did not dare knock on their door or even peek our heads in. We quietly waited for someone to let us know what we should do.

Caleb eventually emerged from the delivery room with baby Hazel in his arms, wrapped in the familiar thin white hospital blanket with its pink and blue stripes. As he handed the little bundle of joy to Jammie, he told us Darcie wanted us to be able to hold her, but he also asked us to stay in the lobby. She was not yet ready to see Hazel in our arms.

Caleb returned to the room before returning soon afterward with a small bottle of baby formula out for us to feed her. This was a complete surprise to us. This was our first indication that Darcie was no longer planning to breastfeed. Jammie and I took turns feeding her.

Caleb sat with us. Even though I had been standing next to him most of the time in the delivery room, the circumstances had hardly given us time to have a conversation. Talk was a little slow and dry at first, but when we found that we both shared a love of playing guitar, words began to flow pretty easily between us. As we dabbled in other topics, we could feel he truly cared about us. It was refreshing to get to know the real Caleb. That helped me toss out the imaginary one—the one who would only complicate things.

After about half an hour of holding Hazel in the lobby, Jammie asked Caleb to go into Darcie's room to ask if she would like us to send Hazel back to her. When Caleb returned he told us that Darcie was not ready to have her back. She also was not ready to see us holding her, so we stayed out in the lobby with Caleb while Darcie stayed in her room with her mother.

After an hour passed and she still had not asked for Hazel, Jammie asked Caleb to once again go to Darcie, but this time she wanted him to ask if it would be okay for Jammie to come see her without Hazel. She said yes, so Jammie and Darcie sat together in her room while Caleb and I stayed out in the lobby, talking about guitars and taking turns holding Hazel.

After yet another hour, Jammie rejoined me in the lobby. The nurses decided to let us use one of the empty rooms rather than hang out in the public area. And even though nobody but hospital staff was present in the maternity wing that day, it was nice to have somewhere to retreat to.

Caleb offered to buy us dinner, which meant the world to us. We ate together in our own room while taking turns holding Hazel. Even though I had been dreading the thought of spending any time with Caleb just half a day earlier, I very much enjoyed having him around now. He spoke openly about how much he appreciated us and what we were doing, and we did our best to show him how much we appreciated him too. It was not only a nice change from our first adoption experience, but Caleb's presence was an added blessing.

Just as had been the case when Ira was born, a handful of family and friends called us wanting to come to the hospital to see the new baby. We asked them all not to come, though. The situation was simply too delicate. That, and Jammie and I felt like we were guests at the hospital. It did not feel right to invite our friends and family to someone else's event. There would be plenty of time for them to see Hazel at our own home if she were to be ours.

When Hazel had first been brought out to us, we thought we would only be holding her for twenty minutes. We eventually stopped asking Darcie whether she wanted us to bring her back because she repeatedly assured us that she would let us know. It was not until we'd had Hazel for four and a half hours that we looked up to see Darcie shuffling into our room, walking very slowly, with a light smile on her face. We rushed to her and wrapped our arms around her.

Darcie sat on the bed next to Caleb, opposite where Jammie and I were, and we offered Hazel to her. She turned the offer down. I was already in love with the little girl, but when Darcie turned down the opportunity to take her from me, I felt an overwhelming rush of love and hope. Even though I had been holding little Hazel off and on for the last four and a half hours, the moment Darcie said she would rather see Hazel in my arms than hold her was the first time I felt like I might be holding my daughter.

I pulled the sleeping baby girl into my chest as tightly as I could without waking her, and simply absorbed her presence. Darcie still had not promised us she would choose adoption, but in that moment I felt my bond with Hazel taken to a new level. At any time up to that point it would have hurt badly to have our adoption hopes stripped away, but that moment pushed me into a position where my heart would have been truly broken.

We talked lightheartedly about random topics, which eventually evolved into discussing Hazel's middle name. Darcie asked us what we thought about calling her Hazel May. We loved it instantly. We not only loved the way it sounded, but we also loved that Darcie had picked it out.

The evening began to get late, so Darcie thanked Caleb for being there for her and hugged him goodbye for the night. He set off on his five-hour-long drive home. Darcie's sister then came and we continued to have fun visiting.

Darcie still chose not to hold Hazel.

Eventually it was time for Jammie and me to head home for the night. Darcie then took Hazel from our arms. It had been one of the most eventful days of our lives, and we left the hospital with an incredible amount of love for Caleb and Darcie.

The next day we started off the morning by coming to see Darcie and Hazel again. Darcie was catching up on some much needed sleep when we got there, so we spoke mainly with her mother. We knew she was hurting from the thought of Hazel being raised in a different home. She teared up as she expressed her appreciation for how much we loved Darcie. I was only able to stay for half an hour before heading to work, so I was not able to see Darcie that morning. Jammie stayed for a few more hours, leaving early in the afternoon.

We had started the day filled with hope that we would be adding Hazel to our family. The previous night had ended on such an uplifting note that we could not help but feel optimistic about becoming parents again. As that second day progressed, though, our hopes sank again.

After Jammie left early that afternoon, Darcie told her that she would call if she wanted us to come back for an evening visit. We waited anxiously all day and into the night with our phones in hand, ready to jump in the car and head to the hospital. Our hearts sank as we watched the evening get later and later without her calling. Our minds gravitated toward our fears of heartbreak.

We went to bed without receiving a phone call and without having any idea how Darcie was doing. We wondered how tomorrow morning would go when Darcie was scheduled to leave the hospital. We did not know if Hazel May would be leaving the hospital with Darcie, or if she would be coming home with us.

2-8

A TEMPORARY GOODBYE

Even though we went to bed worried about what the next day would hold, waking up to a new day rejuvenated our hopes. We had expected a phone call the day before that did not come. Our phones did ring the next morning while we were preparing to come to the hospital. It was Darcie. She wanted to know if we could come earlier than we had originally planned. We hurried to drop Ira off at a friend's house and quickly made our way to the hospital.

Over the last two days, the nurses had often come to Jammie and me to ask questions about Hazel's treatment. They wanted to know from us what vaccinations she would be getting, but we insisted that they ask Darcie. Over and over the hospital staff would get upset that we would not make any of those decisions, but it was not our place to decide. We knew we could always have Hazel vaccinated later, after the adoption had gone through, if Darcie had chosen not to do so.

Darcie later told us how much that gesture meant to her, even though it made the relationship with the nurses frustrating.

After arriving—juggling our nerves and excitement—Jammie and I waited in an empty room while Darcie and her caseworker went over some paperwork. We assumed Darcie was planning to sign the papers since she had asked us to come early, but we were still extremely nervous as we quietly waited. The corny court TV show flickering on the television above us did nothing to help us pass the time.

We felt a lot of inner turmoil as we thought about Darcie in the other room. It brought joy to our hearts to think of Hazel being a part of our family, but the act of signing the papers—the very thing that would make that possible—did not signify party time for us. How could we jump up and down for joy in our room if we knew Darcie was heartbroken in her room? Even if she knew what she was doing was right, we knew the separation would break her heart.

We knew Darcie would come to us after her paperwork was finished, when she was ready, and we were willing to wait as long as she needed. Eventually Darcie came in pushing Hazel's baby cart. Jammie and I immediately rushed over to her and we wrapped our arms around her again. We held each other for about a minute before letting go. We walked together back to Darcie's room to gather the rest of Hazel's belongings before heading out.

When Darcie asked if she could hold Hazel one last time, we told her, "Of course you can," assuring her that it certainly would not be the last time. This goodbye was only temporary.

She smiled an uneasy smile and held Hazel close to her.

When Darcie handed Hazel back to us, we expected her gesture to be the climactic moment of the hospital experience— the last thing she did before we all left the hospital. We expected to immediately be able to slip Hazel into her car seat and head home, but the car seat we had brought was broken. We had inspected it before bringing it to the hospital, and it had not been very long since Ira had last used it, but we could not get it to work properly. We had said our emotional good-bye, but being forced to adjust and readjust the car seat forced us all to stand awkwardly together as we tried to sort the situation out. After 15 minutes of fiddling with the straps, the hospital told us they had a seat they could loan us.

Jammie and I carried Hazel to a room where the head nurse picked out a car seat for us to borrow, leaving Darcie and her mom in their room. When we saw that the hospital was going to lend us a seat similar to the one in our car that Ira had been using, I decided to run out to our car to check the sticker on it to see if it was suitable for a newborn.

As if the trouble with the car seat had not made our departure awkward enough, when I stepped out the side door of the storage room out into the parking lot, I happened to exit just as Darcie and her mom came out of the hospital's front door. They had decided they were ready to leave and wanted to do so without another emotional goodbye. So when I emerged from the side door while they came out the front, it made the situation even more awkward. We smiled and waved from across the parking lot before they made it on their way.

After we had solved the problem with the car seat, I was outside bringing the car around. As Jammie was walking with Hazel toward the front doors, she was quickly stopped by a hospital worker who began questioning her about our little girl. After a handful of questions, Jammie realized that the worker was simply alarmed to see a newborn leaving the hospital with someone who obviously had not just given birth—she did not know if Jammie was a baby snatcher or just a friend wanting to take the baby for a stroll.

Once Jammie realized what the issue was and explained the situation, they had a laugh together and we were on our way.

Hazel was in our care, but the adoption process had only just begun. The paperwork Darcie had signed that morning did not relinquish her rights to the child. It only signed over temporary custody to the adoption agency, who in turn allowed us to care for Hazel. Caleb and Darcie had the right to ask for Hazel back at any time.

We drove Hazel May to our home for the first time. We were in heaven.

I had heard people say newborns can smile, but I never thought it actually happened. I always thought those parents were seeing just what they wanted to see, and that newborns only smiled by accident. But Hazel started smiling from the day she was born. She smiled in reaction to things going on in front of her and around her.

The biggest smile imaginable came across her perfect little lips the first time she was placed into her big brother's arms. Ira now had a little sister who was just seventeen months younger. Jammie and I were beginning to feel like we had a daughter, but there was so much to do and still time to pass before everything would be final.

We snapped a bunch of photographs during those first few days, but we did not send any of them to Darcie. Jammie and Darcie had discussed the exchange of photos and decided Darcie would let us know when it was okay to start sharing them with her. She wanted to take some time away for herself. We told her just to heal at her own pace and to let us know when she was ready.

Darcie's caseworker called us during that time to ask if we had sent any pictures. When we said we had not and told her our reasons, she gave us a hard time about it, telling us we were neglecting Darcie. We began to second-guess the way we had been handling things.

Our relationship with Darcie during those first few days was emotional and delicate. We did not want to do anything to overstep our bounds or make her uncomfortable. Even though Darcie had asked us to wait for her to contact us first, after giving it some thought, Jammie decided to send Darcie a text message to ask her if she wanted pictures. Sure enough, she wrote back saying she was not yet ready.

Darcie texted again after a few more days to apologize about not feeling ready for close contact. We were confused about why she would feel the need to do that. We reassured her that the only thing we wanted was for her to be able to heal at her own pace and in her own way. If she wanted photos, that was fine. If she wanted to come visit, that was good too. If not, we were okay with that as well.

We later found out that after we drove the point home to Darcie's caseworker that Darcie would let us know when she was ready, this same caseworker turned around and called Darcie to give her a hard time about keeping her distance. She told Darcie that most women would not be hurting this badly so soon after the hospital and that the pain usually came later.

The nerve of that lady! If there is one thing I have learned when talking about adoption with other people, it is that there is nothing universal about the feelings associated with the process. Everybody experiences things differently. That is true for everybody involved—whether on the adoptive side or the biological side. So, for this woman to tell Darcie that the hurt she was feeling was misplaced—especially at a point in time when she was so vulnerable to another's opinion—was completely out of line. We assured Darcie that she was not only justified in wanting to heal at her own pace and in her own way, but also that the hurt she was feeling was normal.

We had gone through the adoption process once before, but things were very different this time. Just like we had done the first time around, we were again learning as we went.

Brianna had come over for her first visit the day after Ira came home with us, and Darcie did not want to do that. Brianna wanted a lot of pictures and contact, especially in those early days after placement, but Darcie did not. But we were more than willing to roll with the changes in order to give Darcie the tools she needed to adjust. We wanted her to be comfortable with her circumstances in order to build together the foundation of our open adoption relationship.

It did not happen immediately like it had with Brianna, but Darcie did eventually contact us, asking if she could visit.

2-9

THE FIRST FEW WEEKS

A little before Hazel turned two weeks old, Darcie asked us for pictures, which we were happy to share. A few days after that, Darcie asked if she could come for a visit. We had been talking with her a little via phone and text, but we did not completely know what to expect.

When Brianna had come for her first visit, things were very difficult. She was quite emotional and really struggled to put Ira down when it came time for her to go. After Brianna left, we were very worried she was going to change her mind.

We did not know if Darcie's first visit would be similar—if she was also going to have a hard time putting Hazel down. We were not sure if Darcie was only interested in seeing Hazel, or if she would also want to see Jammie, Ira, and me. We wondered whether or not the visit would be uncomfortable, but we had never let a little fear of discomfort scare us away from anything adoption related before, so we were happy to invite her over.

There were a few uncomfortable moments, but they were very minor. Overall I think it went rather well. There were a lot of smiles to accompany the tears as we talked. We stayed up late, enjoying our conversation. It had never been a problem, especially between Jammie and Darcie, to talk openly about difficult and intimate feelings.

Throughout the entire evening I noticed Hazel was getting passed freely between Jammie and me, but Jammie was never offering to let Darcie hold her. That confused me. It was not like Jammie to refrain from letting Darcie cuddle with Hazel. Since most of the communication before the visit had been just between the two women, it seemed like a good idea to follow Jammie's lead throughout the evening.

After dinner and hours of conversation, I finally offered Darcie the chance to hold baby Hazel.

Both Jammie and Darcie laughed. It was not until that moment that they realized they had forgotten to tell me what they had discussed: We would not offer for Darcie to hold Hazel. Instead, we would wait until Darcie asked to hold her. Since there had been times at the hospital when Darcie had preferred not to hold her, Jammie did not want her to feel obligated now if she was not ready. She was welcome to ask for her at any time. That made sense. Hazel was not being kept away from Darcie. Darcie just needed a little more time.

***

All of Darcie's early visits were similar to that first one. We spent the majority of the time in our home talking. Darcie did not choose to hold Hazel very often, and even when she did, she would usually only hold her for a few minutes at a time before handing her back to one of us. If there was one thing I was grateful for, it was that Darcie was both able and willing to express what she wanted and needed. She was able to be straightforward with us.

Our relationship was still developing, but we felt comfortable enough to ask her if she wanted to do a photo shoot with us. Shortly after Ira was born, before Brianna had flown back to Mississippi, we had taken some really nice photos together. Those were displayed on our walls at home and were still some of our most cherished photos.

We did not get the opportunity to include Ira's birthfather in those pictures, but Hazel's birthfather was much more involved in her adoption. As a result, we thought we should ask both Caleb and Darcie if they would like doing a photo shoot with us. They agreed.

It was a little difficult to arrange a time since Caleb was living on the other side of the state, but eventually we were able to arrange it. We went to the home of one of Jammie's photographer friends and set up in her home studio.

The pictures turned out amazing, but the aftermath was not. In hindsight I reflected on how I would have felt if I had

189

been asked to do a photo shoot with Amber a few months after our divorce. What were we thinking!?

The problem with the situation was not that it put Caleb and Darcie back into communication with one another. They had been talking with each other regularly over the past few weeks, which was part of what made us think they would be comfortable doing the shoot together. The problem was what a photo shoot represented.

Every photo was a portrait of what Caleb and Darcie had wanted to build when they got married. The click of the camera was forcing them to reminisce about the hopes and dreams they once had together. The feelings that had been churned up by their time together at the hospital and the weeks following all came to a head that day.

They seemed to be comfortable next to each other before we started taking pictures, but by the end of the shoot the obvious discomfort was overwhelming.

Jammie and I were terrified after that photo session.

We had planned for a short visit before Caleb would need to drive home, so we drove back to our house. Jammie and I quickly brainstormed about how we could help extinguish the uncomfortable feelings our photo shoot had ignited, but when Caleb and Darcie decided not to come into our house, we became lost in what to do.

Jammie and I walked into the house, but Caleb and Darcie stayed in their car to talk things over.

Hazel was a few weeks old by this time and we had spent every minute of her life growing more in love with her. We knew that there were still a lot of things that needed to happen before an adoption could be final, but we felt bonded to her as if she had been born to us. The fear of losing that, even if we had no right to feel entitled to her, was crushing us. Caleb and Darcie were within their rights to change their minds at any moment and Hazel would no longer be in our home.

Jammie and I sat in the living room as we watched out the window at them sitting in Caleb's car. Flashbacks of watching Caleb hold Darcie's hand at the hospital made me wonder if they were considering giving their relationship another try. I knew what it felt like to consider those feelings since I had gone through something similar with Amber.

And even if they did not rekindle their relationship, we wondered if they were contemplating whether or not to change their mind about adoption.

There was only one thing Jammie and I could do, and that was sit and stare at the black Chevy through the bay windows of our living room. Jammie held Hazel tightly to her chest, unable to put her down for her much-needed nap. She sat in her rocking chair, holding little Hazel May as tightly as she could as I paced the floor, keeping my eyes out on the curb where her biological parents were parked.

That is all we did for one of the longest hours of my life.

Finally, their doors opened and they stepped out onto the sidewalk. We watched as Caleb walked around to where Darcie was standing and wrapped his arms around her. They separated and Darcie walked straight to her own car. Caleb watched her drive away before he tucked his hands into his pockets and walked slowly toward our door with his eyes fixed on the ground in front of him.

We had a million questions in our mind, but we were not sure if it was our place to ask any of them. Once Caleb was seated on our couch, though, we had to at least ask something, or we would go out of our minds with worry.

"I know it's not really our place to poke our noses into your business, but can we ask what you guys were discussing?" I asked.

"We just have a lot on our minds," Caleb said. "It's a very confusing time for us."

"Are you rethinking your decision to place Hazel for adoption?" I had to ask.

He nodded. "We discussed that." He shifted uncomfortably in his seat. "At first we were thinking of changing our minds, but the more we talked about it, the more we know adoption is the right thing. And we are not getting back together."

His words did not completely relieve all our worries, but we were able to exhale for the first time in over an hour. We talked for only about ten more minutes before hugging him goodbye and seeing him off. Before he left we gave him the gift we had picked out for him: a pair of cuff links—one with Hazel's initials on it and the other with her birth date. We had already given Darcie her gift—a locket with a picture of Hazel in it. These gifts were not much, but hopefully they were something they could hold onto for a keepsake.

We had hope that we were on a path that would lead us to being parents again. Still, our bumpy road had a major hurdle. If the adoption was ever going to become finalized, Caleb and Darcie would have to sign papers in front of a judge. In Idaho that process normally takes only a week or two, but that was taking longer for Caleb and Darcie. It soon became apparent that their caseworker was dragging her feet on purpose! It took us a few more weeks to figure out why she would do that.

2-10

TRANSITION TO A NEW LIFE

Brianna had appeared in front of a judge about one week after Ira was born. That court appearance was only for Brianna since Jammie and I would not have our turn in front of a judge for months to come. Brianna's court appearance was only to relinquish her parental rights and transfer permanent custody to the adoption agency. Things were different with Darcie and Caleb.

More and more time continued to pass without their caseworker arranging that court appointment. As we saw opportunities to do so come and go more than once, we realized she was doing it on purpose.

As we pieced together the conversations we'd had with her, it became logical to conclude that she wanted to be sure that Caleb and Darcie had enough time to make sure they were solid in their decision to place Hazel for adoption. After all, even though Hazel came home with us from the hospital weeks earlier, Darcie *still* had not verbalized her decision to place with us. We had heard Caleb say it, but never Darcie. We assumed by her actions that she was leaning toward going through with it, but she had not confirmed that yet.

It was torture for everyone to sit in limbo like this. Every day we worried might be our last one with Hazel. We constantly wondered whether or not Caleb and Darcie would get back together, which we assumed would mean that Hazel would return to them. Every moment with Hazel meant we were falling more in love with her, all the while becoming more afraid that our hopes would be dashed.

I am not sure how that stretch of time weighed on Caleb, but we did talk with Darcie about it. It was just as heavy on her shoulders as it was on ours, and we could only imagine what she was going through. Every morning she would awaken to a new day knowing the child that had grown inside of her was living in a different home, and every morning she knew it was not too late to change her mind. Placing Hazel for adoption was one of the most difficult decisions she'd had to make, and every day she did not get her appointment in front of that judge meant that she had to make that difficult decision once again. Every day she renewed her decision, but from our vantage point, making the same decision each day made it harder, not easier. It wore on her.

Finally, after five weeks without a court date, we called Jon—our own caseworker—and voiced our frustrations about the other caseworker holding things up. He was surprised at

196

this news. He got hold of the other caseworker and when he called us back later that day he said it had been a good thing we contacted him when we did. He and Darcie's caseworker were able to schedule a time in court almost immediately. If we had not called that day it would have taken at least a few more weeks.

During those five weeks after Hazel's birth, Darcie had been making a number of trips back and forth to eastern Idaho. She wanted to get back to the same university she had been attending before she and Caleb separated. She also needed a job, and she hoped to get her old job back. In doing so, she would have had to move back near Caleb if she was going to get her old life back.

During this period of time, Darcie came to me on a few occasions to talk about my past with Amber. She wanted to know what regrets I had, how I overcame certain difficulties, and what factors I considered when Amber and I began to spend time around each other again. It was very hard for me to remain neutral during those conversations since restarting her relationship with Caleb would likely mean changing her mind about adoption, but that was exactly what I needed to do.

I liked both Caleb and Darcie—if they wanted to get back together, who was I to say it was a bad idea? After all, one of my closest friends at the time of my divorce went through something very similar, except that he and his ex-wife did reunite and they are perfectly happy to this day. I knew quite a bit about what she was going through generally, but I could not begin to pretend my situation was exactly like hers.

My decisions regarding Amber would have been much more difficult if there had been a child involved.

Jon set up a court date for Caleb in eastern Idaho first. We were finally taking the next step, which would soon be followed by Darcie making a court appearance.

Jon called us that morning after Caleb's appointment in court and we were given a wonderful surprise. Since Darcie happened to be in eastern Idaho at the time, and since she had already been talking with Caleb, she decided to go with him to court. They both signed at the same time. We had been told that it would be nearly a week before Darcie would get that chance.

We later found out that Caleb and Darcie sat together for hours that morning talking about whether or not they wanted to go through with the adoption or get back together. They had made up their minds before, but this court appearance would make it is nearly impossible to reconsider their decision.

If Jammie and I had known they were together that morning deciding whether or not to change their minds, we would have been an emotional wreck. Since we did not even know Darcie was in eastern Idaho at the time, we had been going about our day as usual.

***

We felt an immediate uplift in Darcie's spirits after she was able to put pen to paper in front of a judge to sign away her parental rights. Now that she no longer had to make the same difficult decision over and over again, she was able to focus harder on her goal of getting her life back into a routine.

She was not able to get her old job back in eastern Idaho and she needed to find work as soon as possible. I had not realized it at first, but her expertise was in the same field as what my cousin, Devin, did, and he was having a hard time finding someone qualified to fill a job opening. Devin was one of the owners of a hospice company, which was right up Darcie's alley. I called him and before long she was sitting across from him to interview for a job. She started out part-time, but soon went to full-time. Getting this job in Boise meant that she was not going to be moving back to eastern Idaho, but she was okay with that. She transferred her college credits to the local university and continued her schooling here.

Devin was an interesting fit into our circle because he was a birthfather, but not really by choice. He was once married and, just like Caleb and Darcie, found out he was going to be a dad about the time he separated from his wife. Devin's ex-wife had done everything in her power to exclude him from his daughter's life. After years of legal struggles and frustrations, Devin eventually agreed to allow his daughter to be adopted by her new stepfather. Devin and I were college roommates throughout the majority of that time and I saw firsthand how it tore him apart.

Jammie and I have always enjoyed open relationships with our children's biological families. We have even grown close to some of the extended family of our children's birthparents. Up until this point, however, we have never had our own extended family interact with our adoptive families. Brianna got to know some of our family while she was living here, but they do not have an ongoing relationship.

We were excited to see Darcie with a good job, but we did not know whether or not her relationship with my cousin, Devin, would complicate things. We knew our relationship with Darcie would have its ups and downs. If things began to go badly at work, would it affect our relationship with Darcie since Devin and I are so close? Would the difficult times in our adoption relationship make it awkward for her at work?

Our worries turned out to be inconsequential. Her new job only helped our relationship as she worked at getting back into the swing of things.

Darcie continued to visit often. We grew closer with each visit. Darcie still did not hold Hazel very often, but their bond grew every time she came over.

Even though we had adopted once before, having a birthparent live nearby was something we had never experienced. A lot of our experiences were brand new to us. Most of the time we spent getting to know Brianna was before Ira was born. After Ira came into our home and our relationship changed, we continued working on our relationship from 2,000 miles away.

We did not have much time to get to know Darcie before Hazel was born, but she lived conveniently close and we were able to spend a lot of time together after placement.

Our situation with Caleb was different. We did not get to know him at all before meeting him at the hospital and although he did not live as far away as Brianna, he did live on the other side of the state. We had been able to visit with him a few times when he was in town, but we decided it was time to take a trip out to eastern Idaho to visit him at his home.

2-11

OUR NEW EXTENDED FAMILY

We called Caleb to see if we could come spend an afternoon with him. He was excited and asked if it would be okay for him to invite some of his family too. We liked that idea and we were excited to meet them.

Car trips had become more complicated now that we had two kids in diapers. We arrived at Caleb's house much later than we had told him we would. When I pulled Ira out of his car seat, I did not realize he had spent the last hour sitting on a really sticky piece of candy. Pulling him out of his seat and holding him close to me slimed my shirt with red goo all the way down my front. And that was nothing compared to the state Ira's clothes were in. It was a warm sunny day, so we stripped him down to his diaper right there on the street and put some fresh clothes on him.

Caleb saw us pull up, and he came out to help sort out the chaos before welcoming us inside. I could not believe my eyes as I stepped into his living room. Jammie and I were expecting to see Caleb's parents and maybe a brother or two, but there was also Hazel's birth great-grandma, a handful of aunts and uncles, a great aunt, and some cousins. Caleb's small apartment was completely full of people anxiously waiting for our arrival and excited to meet Hazel. We felt like celebrities walking in a parade with so many people excited to see us, with all of the love and admiration radiating our way.

People took turns feeding, burping, and snuggling Hazel. We had expected that, but we did not expect the amount of interest they also had in the rest of us. Sure, they all wanted their turn holding the new little baby, but when it was not their turn to hold her, they were just as excited to get to know Jammie, Ira, and me.

They brought gifts for Ira as well as for Hazel. We appreciated him being included like that.

We visited late into the afternoon. As Hazel continued to get passed around, Caleb and I each grabbed one of his guitars and started jamming together. It was fun to finally be able to play together since we had spent so much time talking about it.

A few weeks later we decided to go visit Jammie's brother, who lived only about forty-five minutes away from Caleb. Since the trip would take us through that part of eastern Idaho we asked Caleb if he would like to meet somewhere for dinner. We met for a few hours at a restaurant and enjoyed that evening together too.

All of our contact with our children's birth families had always been on a small scale up to that point—one person here and one person there—that I had not let it soak in just how many people were emotionally invested in our adoptions. Even though I had met some of both Brianna's and Darcie's families before—in person as well as online—being surrounded by so many people at one time really opened my eyes to the magnitude of it all.

Hazel was the first grandchild in Caleb's family. When his mom thanked us over and over again for allowing them a chance to hold her and be part of her life, we were surprised. We had told them we would be doing so, but she said she did not think someone would actually follow through with something like that.

We had already learned to love a birthmother through our first adoption, but having a birthfather in our loving circle was an amazing bonus. When we adopted Ira, because of how things were with his birthfather, we worried ourselves sick all the way up to the day the adoption was finalized. After Caleb and Darcie had their day in court, we did not have much to stress about even though we still had a lot of time before we could finalize the adoption. We were able to spend that time getting to know Caleb and Darcie better rather than worry about thing falling apart.

Our day in court came when Hazel was about three months old.

We expected the judge to be stern and to lecture us because that was what the hard-nosed judge did when we adopted Ira.

Hazel's judge opened the proceedings by looking down at the paper in front of her and saying, "Ooh, and adoption. These are my favorite part of the job!" This judge smiled the entire time we were with her. She was fascinated by the concept of open adoption and spent more time asking questions to satisfy her own curiosity than she did with the actual adoption proceedings. She celebrated our adoption right along with us. Court was not serious and stern this time—it was fun!

I do not think the security guard thought it was quite so much fun, though. He about shut the whole building down when he found what he thought might be a bomb left by the entrance. That was my fault. I put the diaper bag down by the entrance of the building and left it unattended while we were out taking pictures. Oops.

After the adoption was finalized, our relationship with Caleb and Darcie continued to grow. Darcie's visits were usually similar—spending most of the time sitting around talking, laughing, and eating dinner. Even after three months she still did not want to spend much time holding Hazel. That was okay. We wanted her to develop a relationship with Hazel in her own way.

Jammie once asked Darcie if being around Hazel made it hard. Her response surprised me. Darcie said that because three-month-old Hazel looked so different from three-day-old Hazel, that it was like they were different kids. The more Hazel changed physically, the easier it became. I had not thought of that before.

Then a few weeks after the adoption was finalized, Darcie came for a visit and we talked about something that had been on her mind. Her social life was not where she wanted it to be and she thought it might help if she created some distance between us. Her life over the past year had been consumed by divorce and adoption. She hoped that having some time away would clear her mind since over the last year she had thought about little more those two things.

The change would not be permanent. It would be just until she felt like her personal life was back on track. Until she contacted us, we would not call or send text messages. Most importantly, she would not be coming to our home.

We were proud of her for making that decision—not because we were relieved to have her gone, but because she was taking charge of her own circumstance and working through things in her own way. Since one of our main goals with open adoption has always been to give the birthparents the tools they need to heal, we were happy to adapt to these changes. That has always been a big part of what open adoption has meant to us—being open to change.

Although she was not going to be calling or visiting, she still wanted us to share pictures with her.

Sharing pictures with birthparents used to be difficult for us. When Ira was young and we were developing our relationship with Brianna, we felt insecure in our role as adoptive parents. Posting pictures felt like we were reporting to Brianna. Giving her a chance to peek into our home made us feel like we were being examined. The thought of being examined was uncomfortable because, if we felt like we had to report to someone about how things were going, then it was like someone was above us in the pecking order. If there were people above us in hierarchy, then were we really the parents?

Once we had ironed out many of the wrinkles in our relationship with Brianna, we grew a lot more comfortable in our role with her. We were not just proud to be parents, we were also proud to say we were part of the adoption world. When we saw how Brianna supported and sustained us in what we were doing, we stopped feeling so insecure. We no longer felt like we were being audited and it felt more like we were sharing something special with someone we love. I think that is the way it should be.

Since we had already worked out the majority of those insecurities with Brianna, sharing photos with Caleb and Darcie was not so difficult.

Jammie had created a special blog just for Brianna when Ira was born. Choosing to post on a blog rather than send pictures through email or the postal service was beneficial in a lot of ways. Brianna could check the site at her own leisure. She could leave us responses along with the posts. She was able to give the blog password to select family and friends so that they could stay updated too. And since Jammie was a photographer who took very nice photos, Jammie could post them in full resolution rather than shrink them to fit an email or Facebook post. Brianna could print any of the photos at high quality.

After talking to Caleb and Darcie, Jammie decided it would be best to create separate blogs. Caleb and Darcie were no longer spending time together and both wanted to move on with their lives. If they shared a blog, they and their family members would be able to leave comments under each post. We worried it would make them uneasy to be interacting again that way. The last thing we wanted was for their blog to be an uncomfortable place to go.

So Jammie organized and updated three separate blogs—for Brianna, Darcie, and Caleb. Yes, that was a lot of work. Even though Jammie was able to cut and paste most of the information and pictures so that the blogs were pretty much the same, it took a lot of time.

We tried this kind of appeasement for months, having never intended to keep it that way forever. It came to its inevitable end when we accidentally posted pictures of our visit to Caleb's house on Darcie's site.

We then decided it was time to simplify things. We stopped maintaining three separate blogs and merged them into one. We kept our posts neutral, refraining from posting pictures with birthparents, knowing that we could always email those pictures separately.

2-12

ANOTHER VISIT FROM A FAMILIAR FACE

Darcie told us she would contact us when she was ready to start visiting again, but we did not know how long that might be. Jammie and I wondered every day how she was doing. We worried about her because we cared, but we still honored her wishes and kept our distance.

Darcie stayed away for two months before coming over to visit again. Having some time away served her well. She was doing great at her job and made some new friends. She told us it was nice not to think about whether or not she wanted to visit, which enabled her to go about her day without being consumed by adoption. When she started visiting us again she glowed even more than before.

We had asked Brianna on multiple occasions whether or not she wished we lived closer together. She had considered coming out west to go to college, but the more she thought about it, the more she liked having the distance between us. She came to visit around Christmastime when Ira was a little less than a year old, and although there were some difficult emotions during that visit, she loved it. She decided that visiting about once a year would be perfect for her.

Before Brianna's first visit, we stressed about all the things that could have gone wrong. Since that visit went so well we were excited to find out she was coming again after Ira's second birthday. She had always shown us that she approved of our parenting and sustained us as "Mom and Dad," so we were able to let go of our insecurities and truly look forward to her visit.

When it came time for her second trip out to visit us, she was still in high school, which made it difficult to plan a convenient time. We had originally thought about having her stay for a whole week during spring break, but that plan changed: she would fly in late Friday and leave early Monday, staying for a few days over Easter weekend.

Ira had already been asleep for hours when her flight arrived, but she was still excited to see him. It was fun to see her peek in on him to watch him sleep.

Brianna had a lot of fun playing with Ira in the morning as well as getting to know Hazel for the first time. She had been dying to meet her ever since she was born.

Along with being excited to see Ira and Hazel, Brianna wanted to visit with Virginia, who had led the birthmother support group she attended weekly while living with us. They were both anxious to see each other again, so we planned to meet for breakfast that morning.

Even though we had known Brianna for about two and a half years by that point, and she knew us intimately, we still felt the need to prove ourselves as good parents. We wanted to show her with every parental act that she made a good decision when she chose us. She always sustained us, but we found ourselves constantly wanting to prove her right.

When it was time to go meet up with Virginia, I was first out the door with Ira. I strapped Ira into his car seat. As soon as I shut his door and turned to make my way to the driver seat, I heard the familiar click of the car doors locking. I turned back around and saw that I had left my keys in Ira's hand. He had just pressed the *lock* button on the keychain. We did not have a spare. Jammie and I took turns trying to get him to press the *unlock* button on the keychain, but to no avail. Ira spent ten minutes popping the trunk and making the car honk, but he never pressed the correct button. He eventually dropped the keys on the floor.

Waiting for the locksmith to come made us about an hour late for breakfast with Virginia. Brianna was able to laugh about the situation, but it sure was not my brightest moment. Getting the kids ready for breakfast and into the car was one of my first parental acts during her visit and I blew it!

We planned a busy day, which included a trip to the aquarium in Boise. It was a fun activity, but the ride back home sparked a dramatic change to the mood of the visit. Ira was very tired by that point, and like most two year olds, when he got tired he got cranky. His chosen expression of rebellion was to repeatedly kick his baby sister in her car seat. When he

213

was reprimanded he started the biggest tantrum he had ever thrown. He kicked and screamed at the top of his lungs the entire half hour drive home. Brianna was sitting right by him in the back seat the whole time. She was about as uncomfortable as she could be.

Jammie has always been awesome with Darcie and Brianna. She has a connection with them that I will never have. Once we got back home, Jammie could see the discomfort written all over Brianna's face. They knew it was time for a talk.

The last time Brianna had seen Ira, he was not even able to walk yet, let alone talk, so most of Brianna's communication was with Jammie and me. Now that Ira was two years old, he was much more capable of interacting with her. He did not have to roll and crawl anymore because he could walk, jump, and run. He was able to say words, including her name, which sounded a lot like "Banana." He would come up to her, hug her, or jump onto her lap. He was growing up and he was doing it without her there.

Brianna and Jammie talked about something difficult that happened right before going to the aquarium. Jammie wanted to change Ira's diaper before leaving. She called for Ira to "come to Mom." When Ira saw the diaper in Jammie's hand, he ran to Brianna's leg and latched on in hopes to avoid a diaper change. So when Jammie told him to come to Mom, Ira ran straight for Brianna. That sparked some intense emotions that were only fueled later by the discomfort of Ira's backseat temper tantrum.

Brianna and Jammie sat talking in the back room for a long time. Eventually, Darcie showed up and we all ate dinner together. We laughed together as we took a step back and looked at our situation. Many people think we are crazy for letting our children's biological parents be such a big part of our lives. Sitting around the table with birthmoms from both of our adoptions showed how unusual our family tree is, but it has become normal to us. Our home is unique and we love it.

***

The next day was Easter. Brianna had gone to church with us a lot back when she was pregnant, so she was able to see some people with whom she had become friends.

One lady, who was in town visiting her daughter, had heard about our adoptions and was eager to ask Jammie some relevant questions. Her daughter had just finished her adoption paperwork and was now waiting to be chosen. She was especially struggling with the concept that her daughter wanted to parent through open adoption. She struggled to see the benefits of an open relationship. As she asked these questions, she did not realize that the girl sitting next to her, Brianna, was the same birthmom Jammie was talking about. They laughed together when Jammie pointed her out. It was a fun coincidence that this lady had come to visit the same weekend as Brianna. She was able to see firsthand how close, loving, and healthy a relationship can be between an adoptive mom and a birthmom.

After church, Brianna and Jammie packed up all of Jammie's photography equipment and drove downtown for a photo shoot. They had already been planning to take Brianna's high school senior portraits even before Brianna arrived, but did not realize when they planned just how big of a blessing that time together would turn out to be.

Brianna loved Ira. There was absolutely no doubt in any of our minds about that. Still, she needed that break. Having some quality woman-to-woman time together between Jammie and Brianna gave her a chance to relax.

There were a few stressful times, especially for Brianna, but the visit was fantastic. Just like when she had come a year earlier, our relationship with Brianna was brought to a new level. Her relationship with Ira grew as well. It is hard to know how often she will be able to visit over the coming years, or how often we will be able to go to Mississippi to see her, but we are always excited when we get a chance to be together. Our door will always be open to her.

2-13

TOUCHED BY ADOPTION

In the time I have spent as an advocate for open adoption, the question I am asked the most is just how open an adoption relationship should be. This is an intimidating thought for hopeful adoptive parents to ponder. Just like any other kind of relationship, it takes time. That is the most important thing to consider.

Nobody, including the adoption agency, ever told us what our relationship should be like. We invite our children's birthparents into our home because we know it is right for us. A lot of people think we are too open with our children's birthparents. Others think we should be willing to share more than we do. Those people are not in our home and their opinions are not important to us. Jammie and I are the parents and we are the ones God put in this position to make those decisions, not anybody else.

Sometimes, like it happened with our children's birth-parents, relationships blossom quickly. We only needed to sit down with Darcie once before we felt comfortable inviting her to our home. When we thought of the option of having Brianna fly out to stay with us, we hesitated for just a moment to give it thought and then smiled at the idea. We accompanied all of our decisions with a lot of prayer and God was with us every step of the way.

I usually recommend that people start their adoption relationships out slowly—with things they are sure they are comfortable with. It is much easier to start out somewhere safe and secure, not putting too much on the table, and to let things develop progressively. Going backward, starting out with an open relationship then closing some of the communication, is difficult and dangerous to the relationship.

When we were first contacted by Brianna, we did not understand much of what we were getting into. We knew we wanted an open adoption, but we were probably too quick to promise so much. We knew what our pre-birth relationship was like, but we did not realize how it would change.

Before Ira was born, Brianna had all the "power" in the relationship. I do not mean to say she was pushing us around and calling the shots, but at any moment she could have changed her mind and she would have been perfectly within her rights to do so. There would have been nothing we could have done about it.

After Ira was born and the adoption was final, we were the ones in position to call the shots. If at any time we wanted to close the adoption, it would have been within our right to do so. There would have been nothing she could have done about it. The balance of power shifted—the roles swapped. Even during the hard times we have loved having a relationship with Brianna, so cutting her off from contact is not something we have ever considered. Our love for her and her family has always outweighed any of our insecurities.

We were a little wiser as we built our relationship with Caleb and Darcie. There was no way for us to know what our relationship would be like after Hazel was born even though we had been through the process once before with Brianna. We did make promises to Caleb and Darcie, but we kept them simple. We promised them we would never cut them off from contact and we promised we would always be open to discussing what was best for everybody involved.

Also, when we first met them we had a better understanding about the role they would play in our family. Brianna, Caleb, and Darcie do not care only about the children; they care about all of us as a family. None of them visit just to hold the child to whom they gave birth. Actually, in difficult times it seemed like holding Hazel was a safe refuge for Brianna, even though she did not give birth to her. And it seemed to be the same for Darcie when she held Ira.

Our relationships have continued to evolve and we all know that going through different stages in life will mean our relationships could always take different turns. It is likely that Darcie, Brianna, and Caleb will all be married with families of their own someday. Our relationships are mostly based on what we grownups think is best, but someday Ira and Hazel will be able to better understand their situation and will make decisions for themselves. Ira and Hazel may not even want the same thing as one another. Who knows? That is the essence of an open adoption. We are all open to change. We are all open to what other people might need or want. We are all open-minded.

Hindsight has shown me just how much God has guided us through our adoptions. I was not able to see many of the blessings we received at the time, but looking back I can see them plainly.

My divorce from Amber was the most difficult thing I have ever gone through in my life. It beat my emotions up to the point where there were times when I wondered if I would ever feel happy or normal again. But those experiences have ended up being some of my greatest blessings. Although I have always appreciated Brianna, I had never been able to directly relate to her situation. Caleb and Darcie went through something so similar to my own experience that I was better capable of asking myself what it would be like to be in their shoes. The jump between our circumstances was not as far as the leap I had to take in order to relate to Brianna when she was giving birth at age fifteen. I have asked myself countless times how I would feel and react if Amber had been pregnant and wanted to choose adoption. It is helped me see better just how difficult that decision must have been for our children's birthparents. My past has helped me to better appreciate not only Caleb and Darcie, but also Brianna.

I do not doubt God guided us in every step of our journey and He will continue to do so throughout our lives. I do not believe it was a coincidence that our paths crossed with Caleb and Darcie. If we had been just a few weeks slower in deciding to adopt again, or if we had been slower with our adoption paperwork, Hazel would be in someone else's arms.

I trust God. I trust He would have led Caleb and Darcie to another loving home if we were not ready to adopt again. I am really glad we were ready, though, and grateful God saw us as a good fit with Caleb, Darcie, and Hazel. I think we are all a great fit together. Caleb is good for our life and we are good for his. Darcie is good for our life and we are good for hers. Our relationship was not automatic, but it did develop quickly because both sides were willing to share what we truly needed and felt. I am grateful that Caleb and Darcie were willing to let God guide them to us.

When I take a step back, I see just how many people have been directly touched by our situation. My family and close friends, as well as people connected with Caleb and Darcie, will never look at family or adoption the same way. Adoption changes people and it changes lives. One of my goals in life is to help Ira and Hazel see how much love they have brought into the world because of their adoption history and because of who they are. I want them to grow up embracing their past. Whether they choose to speak as freely about adoption as Jammie and I do will be up to them, but in the end they will know just how special they are to all of us.

Jammie and I have benefitted greatly from our relationships with Brianna, Caleb, and Darcie. We did not choose open adoption for ourselves, though. We chose it for our children. As they grow up, their understanding will deepen and they will know that their birthparents made their decisions out of love. They will grow up experiencing that love firsthand because they will know their birthparents personally. They will be able to see Jammie and me demonstrate that love for their birthparents. The best way to teach love is always by example.

Now that I have Jammie, Ira, and Hazel, I have everything I have always wanted. All those years I spent being hungry for the things my brother had are now past; Ira and Hazel have made my life full. I do not know if Jammie and I will ever have another child through adoption or otherwise. I know I am happy, though. Just as I once told my brother as we looked down at his sleeping daughter, I think I am the luckiest guy in the world.

Open Adoption Open Mind

BOOK THREE of the
GLASS HALF-FULL PARENTING PERPECTIVES series

To all the wonderful birthparents out there.
I hope the whole world sees and learns from your strength.

3-1

HIDING WITH THE GOLDFISH

We had only come to the pet store to find a new goldfish, but we found ourselves in quite the predicament when I happened to turn around in time to see Darcie and her husband cross the aisle ten feet in front of me. I froze. This was the last thing we wanted to happen.

Our daughter, Hazel, was five years old at that time and it had been three years since we had last been in contact with her birthmother, Darcie. The last form of communication between us was in the form of a letter she had hand-delivered in the night to our home and left on our doorstep for us to find in the morning. She had not minced words in what she wrote. Although she had previously felt comfortable enough to stop by our home two or three times a week, she made it perfectly clear in her letter that she had no interest in ever seeing or talking to us again.

So there we were, cornered in the back area of the pet store by the fish tanks. There was only one way out of there, which would cause us to have to walk right past Darcie and her husband. Our expectation was that they would quickly find what they were looking for and be out of the store within a few minutes, but that turned out not to be the case. They were obviously in no hurry.

We spent half an hour looking at all the different types of fish and trying to keep our voices down. Half an hour! Young kids can only stare at fish for so long before they begin to get restless, and the inevitable happened.

"Daddy, I have to go to the bathroom," Hazel said.

"You can't hold it?"

"No. I need to go to the bathroom."

We were not scared of Darcie or her husband. We also were not afraid of getting ourselves into an uncomfortable situation. After all, what could be more uncomfortable than hunkering down in the back of a pet store for half an hour hoping we would not be seen?

Our reason for trying to avoid them was because of how we respected and loved them just as much as we always had. As I said before, Darcie had made it perfectly clear that she was not interested in ever seeing us again and we knew that this chance encounter would be uncomfortable for her. We did not want to put her through that if we could avoid it.

I scooped Hazel into my arms, took a deep breath, and started our way toward the bathroom. Any hope of passing them without being recognized was soon gone. I kept my eyes down on the floor as I walked briskly past. I heard Darcie's voice talking playfully with her husband as we passed their aisle, but in my mind's eye I could picture her facial expression when I heard her voice cut off in mid-sentence.

Jammie and our son, Ira, were waiting for us just outside the bathroom a few minutes later.

"Are they gone now?" I asked.

"Darcie hurried out the door as soon as she saw you. Her husband is at the checkout stand right now paying for things," Jammie said.

That moment was really uncomfortable for us, but that day turned out to be another turning point in our adoption story with Darcie. But before I tell how that day changed our path, I should probably rewind back to where *Open Adoption, Open Arms* (book two in this series) left off and recount how we got to this point in the first place.

When that book left off, Darcie had taken a few months off from seeing us to try to get her social life back on track. When she began visiting again, we did not know how often to expect her visits. The location of her new job caused her to drive within a mile of our house multiple times each day. That meant she would have to make the same decision multiple times a day about whether or not to drop in to see us. We had grown so comfortable together that she was granted permission to drop by whenever she pleased, like any other friend. She was coming by two or three times a week at that point—sometimes on her lunch break and other times after work.

There was an innate problem with that. Open adoption relationships, even when they are going well, carry with them an increased intensity. That intensity between us was a good intensity, but it was an intensity nonetheless. When someone stops by for a visit, we would inevitably drop whatever we were doing to give that person our undivided attention. Having that open invitation to stop by without advanced notice created a situation where we were always wondering if she would stop by. Although we loved her deeply, wondering all day every day if she was going to stop by continuously put us on edge. That was not a fun way to live.

When Hazel was a little over a year old, we were invited to a large gathering for Darcie's family. About thirty of Darcie's aunts, uncles, siblings, and cousins showed up to her house for a barbecue. Jammie and I decided we would pull Darcie aside at the end of the evening to discuss our need for a few boundaries regarding visits to our home.

We explained to her our reasons and she said she understood. We gave her the power to decide how often she would like to visit and for how long, but we just wanted those visits to be planned out in advance.

Darcie decided to mull over that decision for a few days before settling on a schedule. A few days later, when she came to our house on another lunchtime visit, she informed us that she had been looking back on how things had progressed in her life regarding the adoption and her personal life and she could see that everything was still revolving closely around Hazel and our adoption situation. She knew she needed to take another break. This time, instead of continuing to receive pictures and updates during her break like she had done before, she wanted to take a break from everything—pictures, updates, visits... everything. Just for a little while. Just so she could break herself from the need to have her life so intertwined with ours.

That was not exactly what we had been going for, but if that was what she needed, then we were happy to honor her wish.

She said she would probably take about three months off, but three months came and went without having contact. When we reached out, she informed us that the time away had been good for her and that she was not quite ready yet to start visiting or receiving regular updates.

It was during that time that she met the man who would become her husband. After about six months of having almost no contact, she sent us a text message saying she would like to see us again and asked if we would like to go out to dinner with her and her boyfriend. We began visiting again, but visits were not nearly as frequent or unpredictable as before. It was nice.

Darcie and her husband chose to have a small wedding ceremony with only close friends and family in attendance. Jammie and I felt honored to be part of that day as we celebrated this big milestone. As we expected to happen, this new chapter in her life also meant that she would pull away a little more.

Open adoption can be really hard at times. As Westley in *The Princess Bride* said, "Anyone who says otherwise is selling something." That first year was definitely the most difficult, but that did not mean that things got easy after that year had gone by.

Somewhere around the time of Hazel's second birthday things were going well with Darcie, but then something happened to cause a rift between us. It must have been something relatively minor because I do not even remember what it was. The real issue was not whatever it was that happened between us that day, but the real issue turned out to be the way we all handled it.

Jammie and I were very busy in the adoption advocacy community at that time. We were running a web page where anybody could come to discuss various aspects of adoption. More than a thousand people would visit our page each day from countries all around the world to take part in a discussion, seek advice and find comradery. We were aware of other similar forums that would only discuss the beautiful sides of open adoption, and some others that only centered on the hot and controversial topics. Jammie and I tried our best to focus on what we considered to be real. We did not want people to believe open adoption was always roses and hugs, and we did not want people to associate adoption only with controversy either. We tried to present a healthy balance of topics where people could discuss the difficult sides of adoption while still seeing its overall beauty.

We posted something about our current struggle on the page with hopes of sparking some good conversation as well as get some quality feedback. That was our biggest mistake. Darcie felt like we were airing our dirty laundry out to the world, and in hindsight it is not hard to see why she viewed it that way. Typing our disagreement onto our page where the world could see it poured gasoline onto the fire. Over the next two days, anything we said only fanned the flames. That was what drove her to write that angry letter—the one that made it perfectly clear that she never wanted to see or speak to us again.

We immediately wished we could somehow take it back, but the damage was done.

Jammie and I were devastated. Her letter pierced us right through the heart because of how much we loved Darcie. We did not want her out of our life and we did not want her out of Hazel's life. We were heartbroken that she not only pulled away, but that she did it so angrily. This was a very different feeling than when she was taking time away to rebuild her personal and social life.

As time went by, I came to wonder if this outcome was inevitable. Jammie and I were not perfect. We never claimed to be. With our relationship being so intensely and intimately intertwined the way it was for those first two years, we were bound to make a mistake. If we had not messed things up that day or in that way, it would have probably been only a matter of time before we slipped in some other way. Through the gift of hindsight, I could see how delicate our situation always was.

Three years went by and we found ourselves cornered in that pet store by the fish tanks hoping to avoid an uncomfortable confrontation. When Jammie and I got back to our car, we sat for a few minutes in the parking lot reminiscing on how much we missed Darcie and wished things could have gone differently between us.

Although we never spoke or made eye contact in that pet store, the incident must have churned her emotions because we received an email from Darcie just a few days later. This was the first time she had reached out to us in any way since leaving that letter on our doorstep. She expressed a desire to see Hazel again, but we could easily tell she had not completely forgiven us for how we had wronged her years earlier. As much as we wanted Hazel to have a personal relationship with her birthmother again, our family is a package deal. The idea of Darcie bonding with our daughter while resenting Jammie and me simply did not work.

In our reply, we conveyed our need to work things out between us adults first. If Darcie was interested, our preference was to begin again by spending a little time together without the children present—perhaps meeting somewhere for dinner—and then later down the road we could discuss face-to-face visits with Hazel again when the time was right.

Our desire to hold off on visiting with Hazel was not solely based on our need for Darcie to let go of her resentment toward us. I will get into this subject more in the next chapter, but Hazel has always been both highly sentimental and very pensive, even at five years old. Hazel missed Darcie. Although her memories of her were extremely limited, she talked about Darcie often. We know our daughter well enough to know that, as much as she missed her birthmom, it would have been much worse to have Darcie come back into her life only to leave again. She would have been devastated.

Darcie did not accept our dinner invitation at that time, but said she needed to consider it.

A few months later, my band performed a two hour set at the county fair in the same small town where Hazel had been born. After the show, we bought a bunch of overpriced carnival ride tickets for Hazel and Ira to squander. As we stood in line for a kiddie-sized roller coaster, I heard Jammie talking to someone behind me.

"Oh my goodness. Can I give you a hug?" Jammie said.

I turned around to see a petite lady looking at Jammie with a confused expression on her face. "Why?" the lady asked.

"Because my daughter is your granddaughter," Jammie said. "It's us. Jammie and Russell."

Her mouth dropped open as recognition set in. "Oh my," she said, and she held out her arms.

We talked for a few minutes before sharing another hug and wishing each other well. I felt bad that Hazel seemed much more interested in the roller coaster she was about to ride than she was in her biological grandma whom she had not seen since before she had learned to walk, but it was a nice encounter.

We kept our eye on Grandma and made sure to approach her for one last hug before we left the fair. This time Hazel was not so fixated on the carnival ride, and by this time Grandma had joined up with Darcie's sister as well.

A few days after that chance encounter, we received another email from Darcie. This time she focused more on catching up on our lives than anything else. She and her husband had a son now. She had finished her nursing degree and was now a full-time RN. She talked about the sweet as well as the sour that had gone on in their life over the past few years. In the end, she said she was not quite ready for visits again (not with Hazel or with us alone), but she just wanted to reconnect through email.

We sent a reply along with some current pictures of our family. Contact has slowly grown more frequent with time. After spending those uncomfortable years apart, we have had to rebuild our relationship anew from the ground up, but that is what we are doing. The days of feeling it would be best to avoid contact by hiding by the goldfish are gone.

During the earlier days after Hazel's adoption, updates had been pretty one-sided with us sharing with Darcie the things going on in our life. Things are different now because updates go both ways. She sends us pictures and updates of her beautiful family as well (she and her husband now have two children).

We still have not met face-to-face since those early days, but recent emails have caused me to believe she has forgiven us for our mistake. The most recent email we received was especially beautiful, expressing how she has come to realize how much she misses us—all of us, not just Hazel. The feeling is mutual. We love her. I do not know when, but I believe the day will come when we are all ready to visit again. We look forward to that day, but we do not want to rush something that important.

3-2

OUR ROCK

Hazel's birthfather, Caleb, has been a rock for us since day one. He has been the epitome of what open adoption should be. And by that, I mean that he has been open to the need for change even when we were sure he wished things could remain the same.

During the first few years, Caleb would make the five-hour drive to come spend the afternoon together before driving back in the evening. He did that a couple of times a year in the beginning. His parents even made the drive to visit us a few times without him. Any time we knew we were going to be in eastern Idaho, we would contact them beforehand and we would get together with him and his extended family.

When Hazel was little, the amount of contact between families was completely dependent upon whatever Jammie and I organized with Caleb. We knew that the day would come when we would need to start tailoring those visits according to her needs, not ours. We did not know at what age that would happen. When it did happen, we did not know if she would express a desire for more contact or less.

The time to make a change manifested itself during the summer after Hazel turned four years old. It happened when we visited with Caleb and his family three times within a five week period.

Those three visits kicked off with Caleb's parents coming to town. His mother is an elementary school teacher and she was required to come to Boise for a training course. They spent the evening with us in our home before leaving to sleep at a hotel.

Months before that visit, we had already planned to make a trip to visit them in eastern Idaho. We expected this visit to be a bigger event than we typically had with them. We invited aunts and uncles and cousins and all sorts of good people. Caleb's parents offered us the guest room in their home to spend the night, which we happily accepted. The evening was full of horseback riding, barbecuing and playing guitar out back by the fire pit.

A few weeks after that visit to eastern Idaho, Caleb's job required he come here to Boise for two days. He spent a little time doing things for his work and a lot of time with us. We filled the day with a fun trip to the zoo. That night we brought out the popcorn and enjoyed a movie. Caleb spent the night on an air mattress in our living room. We cooked a nice breakfast and spent the morning together before he headed back home around lunchtime.

The aftermath of that last visit was quite different than any we'd had with him in all of the previous years.

First of all, when talking solely about how Jammie and I were feeling, it drained us. It had been a few years since Darcie had last visited and Brianna lived so far away that we were not able to see her very often. We had grown accustomed to feeling a bit of distance from our adoptions. Even though we had visited together quite a few times with Caleb, the nature of our relationship still carried an innate feeling of needing to prove Caleb had made the right choice when he decided to place Hazel into our home. As we always did when we were going to have a special guest spend the night in our home, we scrubbed the house from top to bottom. Although he was not asking for much with his visit, we still felt responsible for his well-being, which led to us paying an unreasonable amount of attention to how we thought he was feeling at every moment. Spending so much time together over a five week period brought back old feelings of exhaustion we had not felt around adoption since the kids were younger.

Although we felt fatigued from the intense nature of the relationship, the greater issues that surfaced were those surrounding Hazel. She was only four-years-old, which meant she was old enough to realize there was a difference in who Caleb was—someone different than any other person in her life. Her uncles all adored her, but they did not dote on her quite like this. When she was near him, she was not just a little girl, she was a princess.

It was not hard to see it begin to go to her head. Not only did she pick up on the fact that Caleb treated her differently than any other man in her life, but she also perceived that Jammie and I treated her differently while he was near. Few things are as uncomfortable for parents as having to deal with an all-out tantrum in the presence of birthparents. Especially while Caleb was still in our home, as all young children would do, she began to push the boundaries as far as she could to see what she could get away with. But it did not stop after he went back home to eastern Idaho. She was insufferable for at least two weeks after those three visits. That was not her nature. She had always been such a sweet-hearted little girl.

On top of how the environmental contrast pushed her to behave differently than she typically did at home, I found myself battling different emotions than I was accustomed to feeling regarding Caleb. There was nothing wrong with him treating her like a princess. That was expected. It was hard for me to watch Hazel prefer that over the relationship she and I had. She had always been a very affectionate little girl. When she let go of my hand at the zoo to run up to Caleb and slip her hand into his, I felt a jolt of jealousy that I had never felt around him before. If that were to have happened only once or twice during the visits, I doubt it would have affected me very much, but it happened often during every activity as well as during down time. In the back of my mind, she was supposed to always prefer my hand over anyone else's (except Jammie's, of course).

242

I loved Caleb. I did not enjoy feeling this way around him. Those contrasting feelings beat me up as his presence pulled me in two different directions. Those feelings had not surfaced like this when she was younger. This was new to me.

As difficult as those aspects were, however, the greatest concern for us manifested over the following weeks. As I mentioned earlier, Hazel was a pensive little girl—especially for a four-year-old. She would periodically come to Jammie or me with the types of questions a young girl could not possibly understand.

"Who is Jocelyn's birthdad?" she asked one day.

"Jocelyn doesn't have a birthdad like you do," Jammie said. "Jocelyn's dad is Uncle Clark."

"I know her dad is Uncle Clark, but who is her birthdad?"

"Not everybody has a dad and a birthdad like you do. Most people don't."

Explaining the concept of birthfather proved to be more difficult than we had anticipated. We had been able to explain adoption and birthmothers by telling her that she had grown in Darcie's tummy but that Darcie was not ready to be a mother at that time. We told her we were not able to grow a baby in Jammie's tummy because "Mommy's tummy is broken," but we wanted to raise kids more than anything in this world. This simple explanation brought adoption and birthmothers down to her level and she was able to accept it in her own way, but it still did not explain Caleb.

It seemed the more we tried to explain Caleb without getting into the birds and the bees with a four-year-old, the more we confused her. But most of her questions were not in regards to the "hows" of a birthfather, but focused more on the "whys." Why was she so special to him? He did not live nearby like Uncle Clark did. Why did he did not have any other kids if he loves kids like he does her?

Hazel has a tendency to laser focus her mind on concepts she cannot understand or which unsettle her. The concept of birthfather did both of these things.

For example, a while later, after she began attending public kindergarten, she came home from school with a solemn look on her face. Her personality is typically very bubbly, so it was not hard to notice something was weighing on her as she sat quietly during dinner.

"Mom, Dad, is Santa Claus real?" she asked.

In our home, we like the fun of having Santa Claus be part of our Christmas. We wanted to keep that tradition for at least a couple more years.

"What do you think, Hazel?" Jammie said. "Do you think he is real?"

She pondered for a moment. "Yes."

"Then that's what matters," Jammie said.

"But Gracie says he isn't real," Hazel said.

"It's okay if Gracie doesn't believe Santa Claus is real," Jammie said. "She's allowed to believe that. But we get to believe what we choose to believe, and so in our home Santa Claus is real."

I am sure that type of conversation happens every December in homes all across the globe, but Hazel could not leave it there. The next day she came home from school with the same question, which sparked the same conversation. And the next day. And the next day. Each day the weight on her shoulders seemed heavier than the day before.

We finally decided we had better bring both kids in the living room for a talk. We brought Ira in on the conversation too because we felt it would have been weird telling Hazel that Santa Claus was not real while her older brother still did not know.

"Kids, do you believe Santa Claus is real?" I asked.

Hazel shrugged her shoulders.

Ira said "yes" in such a way that made it clear he was thinking, "Of course he is. Duh. What kind of stupid question is that?"

"Well, we can see how the idea of Santa Claus has been stressing Hazel out lately, so we decided now was the time to tell you the truth about him."

Hazel's eyes grew wider while Ira looked at us with that facial expression of complete confusion.

"Santa Claus is a tradition around Christmastime that is supposed to be a fun tradition, but we can see that it is stressing you out too much, which kind of sucks all the fun out of it." And we went on to explain the truth about Santa Claus.

This experience with Santa Claus was similar to trying to explain Caleb, except that there was no way of finally breaking the news and telling her the truth once we decided she had stressed over it enough. We tried coming at it from a slightly different angle every time she brought it up, but each conversation brought the same result: confusion. A lot of the time she would simply walk away in the middle of the conversation, sometimes while we were still in mid-sentence. I distinctly remember one day when she cupped both hands over her ears and said, "My ears hurt," before turning to walk away.

Having had her in the presence of Caleb and his family so much over a five week span meant that her questions and emotions had not been given sufficient time to simmer back to normal before being around them again.

The fact that Ira's birthmother was still a part of our lives but Darcie was nowhere to be found only boggled her mind more.

It was clear to us that we had pushed her four-year-old brain too far that summer. Open adoption can be very difficult in that aspect. We have to figure things out as we go along. Each relationship with birthparents and their families is different. Ira and Hazel both conceptualize and react to the idea of adoption very differently. Ira did not stress about adoption or birthparents in the same way Hazel did, not even when Brianna came to stay with us for a weeklong visit. All we could do was try our best to do what we felt was right for our children and for our family, and then make adjustments as we went.

One difficult part about this situation was that we had grown quite comfortable around Caleb and his family. They have always been wonderful to us. Having such an open relationship with them made it difficult for us to come out

246

say we needed to pull away from them for a little while. To Caleb, this had to feel like he had been blindsided. That was never our intention, and although we made an attempt to explain our reasons, I doubt he fully understood. How could he understand without being there to watch her turmoil over those weeks following his visits? Still, he honored our wish.

After making that request, we could sense his hesitancy over the next few years. He has always been the kind of man who would not want to step on our toes or ask for something that would make us uncomfortable. Consequently, the fact that we told him we had to take a step back meant that it was hard for him to know where things stood at all times. Any time he asked for anything, he worried whether or not he was asking too much.

We still visited together. We still made the five hour drive out to see him and welcomed his large family to the event, but we did not stay overnight with them and we did not do it quite as often.

Caleb has progressed a lot with his life over the last few years. We are very proud to call him part of our family. He graduated from college and has a great career going for him. We were elated when we found out that he proposed to his girlfriend. We had been able to meet her on a few occasions and they are perfect together.

When we pulled back on visits, we knew it would be temporary. Now that Hazel is a little older, she is processing things better than when she was four. We expect to see Caleb a little more this coming summer than we have over the last few years. In our church, children are considered old enough to choose baptism once they reach eight-years-old, so we have already invited Caleb and his extended family to the event. Caleb has also invited us to come his way to be part of his wedding.

Our goal has always been to attempt to be as consistent as possible. Unfortunately, as has been the case with Caleb, consistency is sometimes too much to ask for in an open adoption relationship. We had found ourselves wanting to be more and more open with time, but there came that summer when we realized we had pushed that relationship a bit too far and had to backtrack for Hazel's sake as well as our own.

Right now things are as healthy and well-balanced as ever. As bouncy as the ride has been, the one consistency in the whole ordeal has been Caleb. He has been our rock, and we are eternally grateful that he has the ability to always be that for our Hazel May.

3-3

AN EVERCHANGING AND
UNHEALTHY RELATIONSHIP

When the second book of this series wrapped up, we still had not been in direct contact with Daren. The last time he was part of our story was when he surprised Ira's birthmother with court papers. Those legal issues fell flat almost as soon as they began, but that part of our story sure shook us up. And to top it off, the last we had heard anything from him was because he was still going out of his way to harass Brianna.

Our plan was never to keep him out of our family. We reached out to him a handful of times but eventually gave up. That all changed when Ira was about four-years-old.

Daren's mother emailed us and asked for some pictures. She also asked if she could be one of our "friends" on Facebook. Our preference since the early days of our adoption story had been for contact to be centered around our children's biological parents and nobody else—not around any of their friends or even their close family. So, the fact that this was Daren's mother contacting us and not Daren forced us to make a decision: We would need to turn her away and say that Daren would be the one who needed to ask for updates, or we could break from the way we had always done things. Our reasons for doing so were laid out in greater detail in the first book of this series, but suffice it to say that open adoption is complicated enough as it is. Steering around the birthparents to communicate with other people only served to complicate the situation even further.

We decided to break from our norm. Jammie accepted her Facebook friend request and sent Daren's mother some pictures and updates. Receiving those pictures must have overloaded her emotions because things exploded immediately afterward. I cannot understand why she would think this type of behavior would be tolerable, but she immediately began writing nasty messages about Brianna all over her Facebook page. That was unacceptable. Nobody talks about our Brianna that way.

So that was it. We told her we had already broken from our norm when we decided to bring her into our circle without Daren wanting to be part of it as well, and the only thing she did was prove why we had made that decision in the first place.

We had no more contact with Daren or his family for about another year before something very unexpected happened: Daren began to show interest in Ira and in our family. Even more unexpected than that was that he contacted Brianna with an apology. I had always figured he would want to have some sort of contact with us someday, but I never expected him to apologize to Brianna for how things had gone in their past.

Brianna wrote to us and informed us that he had asked for our phone numbers so he could send us a text message. We were taken aback, but the fact that he was showing signs of maturity as well as a greater ability to be respectful piqued our curiosity, if nothing else. Our response was to ask Brianna how she felt about it, to which she responded with an open mind.

Over the next few weeks, we shared a little about ourselves, including pictures of Ira and our family. Within a few weeks of that contact, we reached out to Daren's mother and offered her pictures as well. Now that the door was open between us and Daren, we felt a little more comfortable with the idea of having other relatives in on the mix. Of course, we also made it crystal clear that Brianna was our girl through and through, and we would not tolerate the type of disrespect we had seen last time we were in contact. She agreed.

Daren was in his early twenties now and no longer lived at home with his parents. He had just become father to a baby girl. I think the shock of having a new baby in his arms jolted his mind into thinking about Ira in different ways than he had in the past.

That line of communication with Daren stayed the same for a few years. We randomly exchanged text messages. We sent pictures via email. We uploaded pictures and updates to a blog for him to download and print. We connected with him as well as a few of his close family on Facebook.

I could never say we got to the point of having a fully open or close relationship with Daren like we have enjoyed with Brianna, Caleb or Darcie, but it was nice while it lasted.

Everything came crashing down one morning.

It began with Jammie sending Daren a text message to wish him a happy birthday (text messages were his preferred form of communication). His first response was confusing, followed by another one that sent our minds spinning. He began asking Jammie inappropriate questions about herself.

"It kind of sounds like he doesn't realize who he's chatting with," I said as I stared at her phone.

"Do you think that's it?" she asked.

I shrugged. "Probably. You didn't sign your name on any of the texts. I think he thinks you're someone else."

Jammie texted Daren again to ask if he realized who she was. He responded, "Of course I do," and proceeded to ask another question that was even more inappropriate than the previous one.

She texted back again, this time asking if he was high.

He said he was not, and before too long he asked if she would be willing to send an inappropriate photo of herself. We could not believe what we were reading.

"I still don't think he knows who he is talking with," I said. "Nobody is that stupid."

So Jammie texted again. He beat around the bush a couple of times before Jammie insisted. "Prove to me you know who I am. How do we know each other?" Jammie texted.

"You're Ira's mom," Daren texted back.

That was all we needed to know. Any respect we had for him was gone. And just as bad, we could not help but feel like any respect he had ever claimed to have for us was only an act.

I know I should have probably been crazy mad at Daren that day, but all of those feelings were overshadowed by pity. How sad that a man's mind could be that distorted that he would risk throwing away an important relationship for something like that.

We closed that door for a while, but have since allowed it to be cracked open again. We have sent a few updates and pictures since then, but we are not connected on Facebook anymore. We also have sent his mother a few small things here and there, but contact is not frequent or extensive with any of them.

I suppose anything is possible in the future, but I do not expect to ever have a close relationship with Daren, and I do not expect him to be much of a positive influence in Ira's life.

3-4

SO GROWN UP

In just a few months it will have been ten years since Brianna first contacted us. She was just a child back then who found herself in a situation that required her to play the role of an adult. She played the part well, but I must admit I toned down her immaturity when I wrote the first book of this series. I don't say that to sound mean. In no way was she a bratty or bad teenager, but she was definitely still a teenager.

As all birthmothers do, she sacrificed her own instinctive will when she handed that beautiful little baby to us. We watched her heart break in two, leaving half of it here in Idaho while taking the other half back to Mississippi. We naturally felt guilty about that. We wished we could take that away. We ached along with her.

Teenagers tend to mature quickly, so every time she came to visit it was like we were dealing with a new Brianna. For an adoptive couple like us, one of the greatest gifts she could possibly give us would be to allow us to watch her mature and progress in life.

Brianna flew out to see us once a year for the first handful of years. Sometimes she would come alone. Other times she came accompanied by a family member who was excited to meet us in person. I was especially fond of the visit when Ira was three and Brianna brought along her own father. He had been extremely opposed to the idea of adoption when he first learned she was pregnant, but he has been solid over the years. It was a joy to have him in our home for those days.

Through the gift of hindsight, I look back on how wonderful another particular visit had been that seemed like a disaster at the time. Ira had come down with a high fever just as Brianna arrived to town. We had planned all kinds of activities and adventures for those four days, but all of those ideas were squashed by the need to stay home with our sick boy. The reason this turned out to be a blessing was because we could see how much that snuggle time meant to Brianna.

Ira has always been highly active. He was never one to just nestle up next to someone like Hazel would do. Especially when he was younger, he was not much of a snuggler. So this was the first time since he was an infant that she could just wrap her arms around him without him becoming restless after sixty seconds. Since we had become so secure in our relationship with Brianna, it was a delight to simply watch them cuddle up together and stay that way through an entire movie. I guess we learned during that trip that some of the greatest joys in life are found by slowing down and merely appreciating each other's company.

That fifteen-year-old who wrote us that cute letter almost ten years ago has matured into a remarkable woman. She graduated from high school with stellar grades and went on to study nursing. We have always found it funny that the birth-mothers of both of our children chose the same career path. Brianna has been married for a couple of years now and has since left Mississippi. They now live in Virginia.

Brianna and Jammie have become even closer as years have gone by. While adoption was the thing that brought us together in the beginning, they regularly talk over the telephone just like sisters, and oftentimes adoption never even comes up in their conversation. She has always been a beautiful part of our family. We are excited to see what the future has in store for Brianna and her husband, and we love that we get to be part of her family as their story unfolds.

3-5

A LIFELONG CALLING

As Jammie and I were going through the adoption process, we saw the need for more adoption advocacy in the world. We felt strongly that God was calling us to be out there to help educate people on how difficult the adoption process hurdles are. I do believe that it is a good thing there are so many hurdles in order for parents to adopt. If that were not the case, our nation would have a lot more trouble with child trafficking. But why does adoption have to be so extremely expensive?

Along with helping to bring awareness about the difficulties of the process, we have felt like God has called us to be a voice for the beauty and challenges of open adoption. Most people I run into do not have a realistic grasp of what open adoption is like. How could they? It is such an unusual lifestyle that those who have not been closely connected to it could not possibly understand. We did not understand before we got involved either.

That feeling of being called to speak led me to write out the story of our first adoption experience. To be completely honest, I did not have plans to do anything with that manuscript when I wrote it. Within a month of finishing the first draft, I was at an author's convention with a different manuscript in hand hoping to find an agent or publisher interested in my new fiction novel (I write fiction under the pen name N. G. Simsion). I was able to catch the attention of one publishing company's CEO while she was taking a coffee break between classes. It did not take very long before she rejected my novel, but we continued with small talk after my pitch. As it turned out, she had a soft spot in her heart for adoption because of her close connection to it. I mentioned to her that I had written out our experiences after adopting our son and she told me I should bring it to her on the second day of the conference.

To say that manuscript was still a rough draft would have been an understatement. I spent all evening and late into the night getting it a little bit closer to being presentable, but by the time I handed it over to her it was still a mess. To make a long story short, the CEO read the manuscript and was about to reject the book outright, but the lady in charge of marketing talked her into giving it a shot. This put Jammie and me on a whole new pathway because I now had a team of people coaching me on how to reach a maximum number of people through activism. Releasing my book was only a part of the way we reached the community.

I got to know a lot of wonderful people as I sat on discussion panels and taught adoption education courses. Although

Jammie is not a birthmother, she worked with caseworkers to help organize and facilitate birthparent support groups.

The day our relationship with Darcie went into a tailspin by posting too much information on our web page was the day we began to pull back on our public advocacy. We had been living and breathing adoption nonstop for three years straight. Because discussions on our web page could quickly and often get heated, we had to keep a perpetual eye on how the discussion of the day was going in order to make sure our page maintained a welcoming atmosphere—all day, every day. Once or twice a month we were preparing for teaching a class or helping to organize a big adoption event with a local charity.

We were doing all of these things on top of navigating our own complex adoption relationships and figuring out how to be good parents. We had known when we began that we could not do it forever. When we had started, we did not know how long we would ride that exhausting advocacy train, but we knew we had to keep a close eye on whether or not it ever over-powered the aspects of adoption that were most important to us: our children and their birthparents. When Darcie left that scathing letter on our doorstep, we knew we had pushed that envelope too far and it was time to pull back.

We felt good about the timing of this decision from the amount of attention our web page required. Since we had put so much time and tears into that page, we were not about to let it fade into nothing—not after all the good it had been able to accomplish over the last few years. We prayed fervently about what to do with it, and we both knew there was only one person we trusted to take over. She has done an amazing job at serving the adoption community by keeping that page going over the years.

Over the next year and a half, we continued to be part of the adoption advocacy world by participating on panel discussions and teaching a class here and there. When our adoption agency made some needed changes to their programs, we decided that would be our time to pull back even further.

Although it had been a mistake we made with Darcie that first changed our adoption advocacy path, our main focus regarding advocacy had always been to monitor how it would affect our children. The larger our audience grew, the more we knew our advocacy could push them into a spotlight they may or may not embrace. That would have been the last thing we wanted.

On top of that, our plan has always been to ensure our children feel like they are in charge of their own adoption story. During their first few years, we made all of the decisions based primarily on what we felt best. As Ira and Hazel grew a bit older and they began to react and interact more, we have had to reanalyze our focus. Now, we always ask for their input when we are making decisions regarding their adoption relationships. Our goal has always been to prepare them for the day when those reins are handed over to them so they can make all of those decisions on their own.

Ira and Hazel process their situation very differently. Hazel thinks about her birthparents often and brings them up in conversation regularly. Ira is not like that. He enjoys the little things, like when Jammie hands him her cell phone to send Brianna a happy birthday text message or a quick video chat on Birthmother's Day (the day before Mother's Day), but he does not spend nearly as much time thinking about these things as his sister does. In fact, it was not until just about two months ago that Ira walked into our room late in the evening and asked, "What is my birthdad like? Have you met him?"

Ira has a picture of his birthmother on his dresser next to his bed, and Hazel has pictures of her birthmother and birthfather's whole family, but we do not have a good picture of Daren for his dresser. Ira has never had a text message conversation with Daren or visited with him on a video chat.

For thirty minutes, Jammie sat cross-legged with him right there in the middle of the floor and had a beautiful heart-to-heart about anything he wanted to discuss regarding adoption. We had always tried hard to make sure he knew the door was open for that discussion, but, unlike his sister, this was the first time he ever instigated it on his own. I sat on the edge of the bed and offered my feelings here and there, but I mostly just smiled at the sight of them sharing this moment. She talked to him about how he has two younger half-sisters now through Daren's side. She talked about some of the good things Daren has done and sugarcoated some of the reasons why we have not been in contact much with him over the years.

As unfortunate as our relationship with Daren has been over the last few years, this moment with Ira made me glad that door has remained open a crack. Someday Ira will be old enough that he can decide for himself what he wants to do with that relationship, but that will be another hurdle for another day.

3-6

THIS IS WHO WE ARE

A fifteen-year-old girl we knew from church came to us one day and told us she was pregnant. She hung her head low as she said, "I was raped. I want you two to raise my baby."

We stood there with mouths agape as she talked about all of the terrible things going on in her life—how she was being abused at home where she lived with her grandma and uncle, the way the boys were verbally attacking her all day at school now that she began talking publicly about her rape, and her need to get out of the situation she was in. What a mess!

We took her straight to one of our church leaders to help sort out the situation. By the end of our discussion, we decided on a plan to get her out of there. Jammie and I agreed to allow her to stay in our home for a week as we sorted through some long-term options.

We knew from the start that we were not going to adopt this girl's baby. As soon as she began pouring out her soul, we knew that the adoption relationship that would be built upon this foundation was going to be incredibly delicate and even more complex than those we already had. We felt our role in this story would be to remain close to her through it all and we learned firsthand how important it is for us to have a bit of personal space for the adoption relationship to remain healthy. That would be too difficult to navigate while living a block away from all of this girl's family. On the other hand, our time as adoption advocates meant we knew of many wonderful couples right off the top of our head who would be over-the-moon excited to adopt this child and were strong enough to handle such a complicated situation.

I remember like it was yesterday the moment we all stood in the living room of that young girl's grandmother to have an intervention. Telling this grandma that her home was unfit for raising a teenager was one of the most uncomfortable things I have had to be part of. I knew this woman—not well, mind you, but we attended the same church. I did not know whether to be angry with her at the life this teenager was enduring or to feel sorry for her when I saw the hurt in her eyes.

We left that house with enough clothing for a week and drove straight to our house.

We tried our very best to give her the best emotional support possible. Jammie encouraged her to attend the same birthmother support group Brianna had attended when she was expecting Ira. Within a few days, however, it became apparent that Jammie and I needed to have a private discussion about our situation.

"How long ago did she say the rape took place?" I asked as Jammie and I walked together hand-in-hand around our neighborhood.

"Two months ago, I think she said," Jammie said.

"That's what I thought."

"Why?"

"Because something is off. I can't say for sure or to what extent, but not everything she is saying can possibly be true. She told me today that the doctor said she was having twins—a boy and a girl. And she said he told her that at her appointment a few weeks ago."

Jammie sighed. "Yeah. That's not possible to know this early in a pregnancy."

"Do you think she is really pregnant?" I asked.

"I have been wondering that myself. It's not exactly the kind of thing you call someone out on unless you're absolutely sure."

"Right." I pondered what to say next, since even voicing these next words on my mind made me feel guilty for thinking them. "At this point, I'm not even sure the rape ever happened."

"Again, it's not exactly the kind of thing we can just call her out on without being sure. The last thing a rape victim needs are more people saying they don't believe her."

By the end of the week, we did end up confronting her about it. We had to. Her story was changing so much that we knew it could not possibly be true. As much as we felt like she played us for fools, the worst part of it all was that she had been dragging the name of one her schoolmates through the mud with this false rape accusation.

She admitted the rape never happened. She admitted she had never been pregnant. The abuse and neglect she said had been happening at home was also made up. When it came down to it, she was just another case of a teenager wanting to get out of the house and live with someone else. Most teenage girls have wished for that at some point in their life, but this one took it to the extreme. She knew we had especially soft hearts for birthmothers and thus could see a way to take advantage of us.

This was the only time someone tried to manipulate us, but it was not the only time our hearts were sent into a frenzy. It was not the only time someone came to us for help with an unplanned pregnancy. Over the next five years, although we had already decided we were finished adopting now that we had two children, we were asked three more times to adopt someone's child. Two of those times we knew it would be best to refer them to one of the other hopeful adoptive couples we knew. The third time we actually agreed to adopt the child, but none of those three adoptions ever took place.

Some people are so shocked by the reality of an unplanned pregnancy that they decide early on in their pregnancy that they need to place their child for adoption. But as those nine months progress, it becomes very common for the mother-to-be to decide to raise the child herself. Adoption has continually become more and more rare.

Especially as political debates have heated up over the years regarding late-term abortions of babies who are mature enough to survive outside the womb, I am saddened by the fact that adoption is so rare. I do not think for a second that all women with unplanned pregnancies should place that child for adoption. I do not think it is right to even suggest that all single women need to consider it, but I sincerely wish adoption was more commonly a part of people's everyday conversation.

The truth is that, for every adoption that takes place, there are ten pregnancies ended by means of abortion. Being a man who sees everything in this world through my adoption lenses, I am saddened by that statistic.

There was a scene in *Open Adoption, Open Arms* in which Jammie and I attended a mandatory adoption preparation class. As we were socializing with some of the other hopeful adoptive parents, I quickly recognized a couple who had been in some of those classes when we adopted our first time around. I made some form of comment to them, assuming incorrectly that they were back to adopt again like we were. By the sad look in their eyes, I knew I had made a mistake even before they informed me they were still waiting to adopt for the first time.

We felt incredibly guilty about that. Many of the couples with whom we attended classes had been waiting since before we adopted the first time and here we were back to do it again.

Years later, I remember very well one afternoon when I was sitting quietly at a desk in the back corner of the public library working on one of my fiction novels. I noticed the familiar face of another woman I had known from the adoption world.

I took my hands off the keyboard and greeted her. "It's so good to see you again," I said. "I have lost touch with a lot of the awesome couples we used to see in our adoption classes since we don't teach them anymore. How are things going?"

She turned her eyes away for a moment before saying, "We took our name off the waiting list. We tried for nine years, but never got selected."

"I'm so sorry," I said. This fate was not new to me. I knew that was the reality for many of the couples we had worked with through our years of advocacy.

"We couldn't see the point in spending a thousand dollars to have our homestudy done every time we needed to renew. But more than that, we just gave up, I guess. A person can only hold onto that hope for so long and feel defeated every time we see someone else adopt."

I wish I could say I had some awesome words of comfort for her that day, but that would be a lie. I felt terrible for her, especially since their profile had been on the list when Jammie and I began the process and were there long after we had successfully adopted twice. I do not think the average person realizes how many couples give up after years of trying. Over that final year when Jammie and I were working closely with one of our local adoption agencies, there were eighty couples in the state of Idaho hoping to adopt through that agency. Only twelve adoptions took place that year.

We do not spend time monitoring a discussion board on a web page like we used to, but we feel like our calling to be adoption advocates is a lifelong pursuit. That call to act will manifest itself in a variety of ways as we pilot our family, but we will never keep our mouths closed.

There have been many times in our life when we have wished we could just be normal, but "normal" is not in the cards for us. There is a reason we have pictures of our children's birth families displayed in our home. They are family and we love them, and not only when times are easy.

Our family tree is unique. This is not only what we do. This is who we are.

Russell and Jammie's First Adoption Profile letter:

We can't begin to tell you how much love and respect we have for every birth parent who makes that difficult decision to place a child for adoption. We have been unable to have our own children, so we're incredibly grateful for people like you who are willing to help us realize that dream. Thank you for making that decision, and thank you for taking a moment to get to know us a little bit by reading our letter to you.

About Us

Our story began on a Sunday morning in church. With a little over a year left in college, Russell had just moved into a new apartment. Jammie had just moved to town a few days earlier and was staying with her parents while she looked for her own place. The timing couldn't have been any better. If Russell had moved to his new apartment a few weeks later, Jammie would have already been living in her new apartment fifteen miles away. If Jammie had moved to the area a few weeks earlier, Russell wouldn't have spent that first Sunday at church with his eyes glued to the beautiful blonde across the room. It didn't take Russell very long to have her cornered as he introduced himself and found out her name. All of the usual steps of dating and going home to meet each other's family soon followed, and before long, Russell was nervously in front of Jammie's father asking him for his blessing to marry his daughter.

Jammie was born in Utah. She grew up being the only girl and the youngest sibling in the house until her younger sister was born when she was 11 years old. She would spend part of the day roughhousing with her three older brothers and then the rest of the day playing on the floor with her baby sister. She doesn't wrestle with her brothers anymore, and her baby sister is now a young teenager, but it's still just as enjoyable to get together as a family.

Russell was born in Maryland and grew up as the fourth child out of six. While the Navy had Russell's family moving around a lot, he spent the majority of his younger years living in Nevada. He loved catching lizards and playing football or baseball with his siblings and friends out in the desert sand. All of Russell's siblings have moved out of Nevada, but everyone is still within driving distance and enjoys getting together as often as possible.

While growing up, Jammie's family watched rodeos and rode horses while Russell's family preferred watching baseball and tossing the ball around. Jammie's dad built saddles and programmed computers, while Russell's dad was a hospital administrator for the Navy. Jammie lived in the same house until she was 17 years old, while Russell lived in 10 different houses before he left for college at age 17. Jammie's house was mostly decorated with a country style, while Russell's house was mostly decorated with paintings and stained glass done by family members. With all of the differences in styles, though, the similarities are much stronger. Both families love to keep in close contact. Both families love to get together whenever possible to ride horses or play softball. Both families would do anything for each other, and both families love each other more than anything.

How We Live

Russell graduated from college with a bachelor's degree in Sociology and also graduated from a technical school with a degree as a dental laboratory technician. He worked for a few years under someone else before he and Jammie started their own dental lab business doing the same thing. At work in the dental lab, Russell does the majority of the work required to make gold and porcelain crowns, veneers, bridges, etc. Jammie assists in the initial phases of the crown-making process by making models of the teeth and also is very good at handling the majority of the business organization and finances, both of which she does from home. We love what we do.

After graduating from college and moving to Boise, we spent the first few months searching for our perfect home. We weren't allowed any pets when we were living in our college apartment, so we were almost as excited to be able to get a dog as we were about getting our own house. On the first day that we could move into our new place, we unloaded one truckload of our belongings and then went to pick out a dog even before we went to load up the second truck. We now have two dogs, Bogey and Mulligan, which we chose because of how good their breeds are as family dogs. *Most of our friends have children, and our nieces and nephews are over all the time, so both dogs are great with kids.*

Our Interests

We're never short of pictures from any event. Jammie loves photography and takes her nice camera just about everywhere she goes. Weddings or family portraits are the most common things that she photographs, but she's done photo shoots with just about anyone or anything, and they all turn out beautifully. The only problem with her photography is that Russell often forgets to take the camera out of her hands, so she's not in as many pictures as he is.

When Russell was a teenager he never skipped a day of practicing his guitar. On most days, he would come home late from working at the grocery store with his body being tired but his mind telling him otherwise. He would tell himself he'd just play for five minutes or so, but he always ended up strumming that six-string well past his bedtime. The many hours of practice paid off. Russell has a band with two of his brothers who play with him on stage all around the Boise area and are currently working on recording their fifth album.

Russell and Jammie both love to be active with all kinds of sports. Russell played baseball for his high school varsity baseball team, so when he married Jammie, she took up the sport and has played on softball teams with him. Jammie played basketball on her high school basketball team, so when she married Russell, he took up the sport too. Russell discovered disc golf (Frisbee golf) a few years before meeting Jammie, so she took up the sport and both have won many tournaments all around Idaho and Utah. Jammie discovered volleyball a few years before meeting Russell, so he took up that sport as well, and they have fun playing together on city league teams or just with other friends. Whatever sport it is, Russell and Jammie have probably tried it and enjoyed it.

No matter what our interest is, we enjoy doing it together. Jammie often comes up on stage to sing a song or two with Russell while he's performing. Russell goes with Jammie from time to time to help her out with a photo shoot. We love to spend the time together even more than we enjoy the activities itself. We are best friends.

Thank You

For four years now we have been trying to have children and start our family. We have been seeing specialists about our situation, but nothing has worked and each month that goes by has left us with more heartache. We can't fully understand everything you are going through during the adoption process, but we want you to know that we respect and love you very much for the decision you have made to provide additional love for your child through adoption.

Russell and Jammie's
Second Adoption Profile Letter read:

We can't begin to tell you how much love and respect we have for everybody who makes the difficult decision to place a child for adoption. We have been unable to have our own children, so we are incredibly grateful and excited about the prospect of adoption. Thank you for taking a moment to get to know us a little bit by reading our letter to you.

About Us
Our story began on a Sunday morning in church. With a little over a year left in college, Russell had just moved into a new apartment. Jammie had just moved to town a few days earlier and was staying with her parents while she looked for her own place. The timing could not have been any better. If Russell had moved to his new apartment a few weeks later, Jammie would have already been living in her place fifteen miles away. If Jammie had moved to the area a few weeks earlier, Russell would not have spent that first Sunday with his eyes glued to the beautiful blonde across the

room. It did not take Russell very long to have her cornered as he introduced himself and found out her name. All of the usual steps of dating and going home to meet each other's families soon followed, and before long Russell was nervously standing in front of Jammie's father asking for his blessing to marry his daughter.

Jammie was born in Utah. She grew up being the only girl and the youngest sibling in the house until, when Jammie was 11 years old, her younger sister was born. Jammie would spend part of the day roughhousing with her three older brothers and then the rest of the day playing on the floor with her baby sister. She does not wrestle with her brothers anymore, and her baby sister is now a teenager, but it is still just as enjoyable to get together as a family.

Russell was born in Maryland and grew up as the fourth child out of six. While the Navy had Russell's family moving around a lot, he spent the majority of his younger years living in Nevada. He loved catching lizards and playing football or baseball with his siblings and friends out in the desert sand. All of Russell's siblings have moved out of Nevada, but everyone is still within driving distance and enjoys getting together as often as possible.

While growing up, Jammie's family watched rodeos and rode horses while Russell's family preferred watching baseball and tossing the ball around. Jammie's dad built saddles and programmed computers, while Russell's dad was a hospital administrator for the Navy. Jammie lived in the same house until she was 17 years old, while Russell lived in 10 different houses before he left for college at age 17. Jammie's house was mostly decorated with a country style, while Russell's house was mostly decorated with paintings and stained glass art done by family members. With all of the differences in styles, though, the similarities are much stronger. Both families love to keep in close contact. Both families love to get together whenever possible to ride horses or play softball. Both families would do anything for each other, and both families love each other more than anything.

How We Live

Russell graduated from college with a bachelor's degree in sociology and also graduated from a technical school with a degree as a dental laboratory technician. He worked for a few years under someone else before he and Jammie started their own dental lab business. At work in the dental lab, Russell does the majority of the work required to make gold and porcelain crowns, veneers, bridges, etc. Jammie stays at home to take care of our son, Ira. She helps Russell with the lab by taking charge of the finances, which she is able to do from home.

After graduating from college and moving to Boise, we spent the first few months searching for our perfect home. We were not allowed any pets when we were living in our college apartment, so we were almost as excited to be able to get a dog as we were about getting our own house. On the first day we could move into our new house, we unloaded one truckload of our belongings and then went to pick out a dog, even before we went to get the second truckload of stuff. We now have two dogs, Bogey and Mulligan, and we chose them because their breeds are great as family dogs. Most of our friends have children, and our nieces and nephews are over all the time, so both dogs are great with kids.

Our Interests

We are never short of pictures from any event. Jammie loves photography and takes her nice camera just about everywhere she goes. She mostly photographs weddings or family portraits, but she's done photo shoots with just about anyone or anything, and they all turn out beautifully. The only problem with her photography is that Russell often forgets to take the camera out of her hands, so she's not in as many pictures as he is.

When Russell was a teenager he never skipped a day of practicing his guitar. On most days, he had come home late from working at the grocery store with his body being tired but his mind telling him otherwise. He would tell himself he had just play for five minutes or so, but he always ended up strumming his six-string well past bedtime. The many hours of practice paid off. Russell has a band with two of his brothers who play with him on stage all around the Boise area. They are currently working on recording their fifth album.

Russell and Jammie both love to be active with all kinds of sports. Russell played baseball for his high school baseball team, so when he married Jammie, she took up the sport and has played on softball teams with him. Jammie played on her high school basketball team, so when she married Russell, he took up the sport too. Russell discovered disc golf (Frisbee golf) a few years before meeting Jammie, so she took up the sport and both have won many tournaments all around Idaho and Utah. Jammie discovered volleyball a few years before meeting Russell, so he took up that sport as well, and they have fun playing together on city league teams or just with other friends. Whatever sport it is, Russell and Jammie have probably tried it and enjoyed it.

No matter what our interest is, we enjoy doing it together. Jammie often comes up on stage to sing a song or two with Russell while he's performing. Russell goes with Jammie from time to time to help her out with a photo shoot. Simply spending time together is the most important part. Russell and Jammie are best friends.

With all of our interests, family has always been number one. Adoption has given us the gift of parenthood, which will always be at the top of our priority list.

Thank You

We can't fully understand everything you're going through, but we want you to know that we respect and love you very much. When that happy day does come and we are able to adopt again, we look forward to having an open and loving relationship with our child's birthparents, similar to the beautiful relationship we have with our son's birth family. We are excited to share updates as well as pictures, building our open relationship as we go. Again, thank you so much for taking the time to get to know us. If you had like to see the current updates on our blog, or if you had like to contact us, you can find us at:

xxxxxxx.blogspot.com
xxxxxxx@gmail.com

About the Author

Russell was born on Andrews Air Force Base near Washington, D.C. Along with his five siblings, he and his military family moved around a lot, living in eight different houses by the time he left for college at age 17. Although his family moved away from Fallon, Nevada, just a few months after he moved out, he still considers that little oasis in the desert to be his childhood hometown.

Russell moved to Idaho after graduating from Brigham Young University in Provo, Utah. He is captain of his men's league softball team, die-hard fan of the Oakland Athletics, avid disc golfer, fiction writer under the name N.G. Simsion, and guitar player/singer with a band he formed with his brother called *The Two in the Middle*.

Above all, Russell loves God and his family.

Printed in Great Britain
by Amazon